WILLIAM CAXTON

WILLIAM CAXTON

AN EXHIBITION TO COMMEMORATE
THE QUINCENTENARY OF THE
INTRODUCTION OF PRINTING
INTO ENGLAND

BRITISH LIBRARY REFERENCE DIVISION

24 SEPTEMBER 1976 – 31 JANUARY 1977

PUBLISHED FOR
THE BRITISH LIBRARY
BY
BRITISH MUSEUM PUBLICATIONS LIMITED

3115

© 1976, The British Library Board
ISBN 0 7141 0388 8
Published by British Museum Publications Ltd
6 Bedford Square, London WC1B 3RA

Designed by Nicolas Barker
Set in 'Monotype' Bembo
Printed in Great Britain by
Balding & Mansell Ltd, London and Wisbech

ACKNOWLEDGEMENTS

The British Library Board wishes to thank those who have generously lent to this exhibition:
  The Curators of the Bodleian Library;
  The Department of Prints and Drawings, British Museum;
  Chetham's Library, Manchester;
  The College of Arms, London;
  The President and Fellows of Corpus Christi College, Oxford;
  His Grace the Archbishop of Canterbury and the Trustees of Lambeth Palace Library;
  The Dean and Chapter of Lincoln Cathedral;
  The Worshipful Company of Mercers;
  The Master and Fellows of Pembroke College, Cambridge;
  The Pierpont Morgan Library, New York;
  The Public Record Office;
  The Dean and Chapter of Westminster;
  An anonymous lender.
Photographs in the exhibition and in the catalogue are reproduced by kind permission of:
  Biblioteca Apostolica Vaticana;
  The Curators of the Bodleian Library;
  Historisches Archiv der Stadt Köln;
  The Huntington Library and Art Gallery, California;
  The Worshipful Company of Mercers;
  The Pierpont Morgan Library, New York;
  The Public Record Office;
  The Uppsala University Library;
  The Dean and Chapter of Westminster;
  Westminster Public Library.
The British Library Board also wishes to thank Mr G. D. Painter, formerly Assistant Keeper in charge of incunabula in the Department of Printed Books, who has kindly made available for the purpose of compiling this catalogue the typescript of his book *William Caxton: a quincentenary biography* (Chatto & Windus, 1976).

FOREWORD

Among the events in the programme of celebrations co-ordinated by the Caxton Commemoration (1976) Committee there are two in particular to which the attention of visitors to this exhibition is drawn: they are the exhibitions on Caxton at the Cambridge University Library and at the John Rylands University Library of Manchester; both of these exhibitions contain a number of unique Caxton items of great importance and are being held at the same time as the British Library exhibition; to this extent the three exhibitions and their catalogues complement one another.

This catalogue has been compiled by Janet Backhouse of the Department of Manuscripts and by Mirjam Foot and John Barr of the Department of Printed Books.

All Caxton's books were printed at Westminster except for the first six which were printed while he was at Bruges. As they had no title-pages the generally accepted titles for them in modern spelling have been used. Spelling has been modernized throughout this catalogue apart from very brief quotations.

Reference has been made wherever applicable to these standard works as follows:

Duff = E. Gordon Duff: *Fifteenth Century English Books* (1917);

STC = *A Short-title catalogue of Books printed in England, 1475–1640* (1926);

De Ricci = Seymour de Ricci: *A Census of Caxtons* (1909).

Undated editions are supplied with inferential dates in square brackets, in accordance with those suggested by G. D. Painter in his *William Caxton: a quincentenary biography* (1976).

A descriptive article by H. M. Nixon on the Caxton editions acquired by the British Library since the publication of De Ricci's *Census of Caxtons* is to be published in the *British Library Journal*, vol. II, no. 2, Autumn 1976.

The best source for present day locations of copies of Caxton editions, including those discovered since 1926, is the revised *Short-title Catalogue* (vol. II, published 1976).

Modern editions, reprints and facsimiles of Caxton texts are listed in *The New Cambridge Bibliography of English Literature*, vol. I (1974) and in N. F. Blake, *Caxton and his World* (1969).

INTRODUCTION

The invention of printing with movable types in the mid-fifteenth century made it possible to produce texts in multiple copies with a speed, accuracy and cheapness previously inconceivable. This revolutionary technique was introduced into England by William Caxton, a successful businessman with literary tastes who had learned to print at the age of fifty or so. He set out to provide his countrymen with the fashionable continental literature of his day in English, often in his own translation.

William Caxton is one of the most famous Englishmen who ever lived. He was the first English printer; while he was living abroad in Bruges he produced the first book to be printed in the English language, the *Recuyell of the Histories of Troy*, which he himself translated from the French. After producing six books at Bruges, including some of the first printed in French, he moved to England in the autumn of 1476 and set up the first English press in the precincts of Westminster Abbey. Our exhibition commemorates the quincentenary of this event.

Although Caxton's fame is largely due to the increasing importance in later centuries of both printing and the English language, his achievements and distinctive character as a printer, publisher and translator are worth examining for their own sakes. Our exhibition accordingly gives an outline of his life and career and shows examples of the greater part of what he printed, supplemented by examples of contemporary book-production in manuscript.

(20), *p.38*

Caxton's earlier career

William Caxton was born, probably about 1422, in Kent and in June 1438 was apprenticed to a Mercer in the City of London. Around 1445 he went to Bruges to take part in the trade there of the Merchant Adventurers of whom the London Mercers were prominent members. In 1452 he took the livery of the Mercers' Company; in 1462 he became Governor of the English Nation at Bruges and engaged in various diplomatic negotiations on behalf of Edward IV. After Edward's exile in 1470–1, Caxton seems to have lost his post; another Governor was appointed and Caxton made the change in his career for which he is remembered.

He moved to Cologne and finished there the translation he was making under the patronage of Margaret of York, Duchess of Burgundy: the *Recuyell of the Histories of Troy*. It was during his stay in Cologne that Caxton learned to print. In 1475 he was operating a printing press in Bruges with a local scribe and bookseller, Colard Mansion, on which he printed first the *Recuyell* and then other books in French and English. In order to carry his new business into England itself he rented premises at Westminster, the seat of the court and parliament. The first surviving piece of print he produced there was the Indulgence of which a unique copy, dated 13 December 1476, was discovered by A. W. Pollard in 1928 in the Public Record Office.

The invention of printing

Printing was invented at Strasburg in the late 1430's and perfected at Mainz in the early 1450's by the Mainz goldsmith Johann Gutenberg. His invention consisted not merely of impressions from movable inked letter-forms, but also of the techniques of making them efficiently: its new features included an adjustable hand-mould with a punch-stamped or engraved matrix in it, in which type could be cast in large quantities; a type-metal alloy (probably lead with tin and antimony) combining a low melting point with the property of rapid, undistorted solidification on cooling; a hand-press adapted from the presses used by papermakers, bookbinders and others; and an oil-based printing ink.

The early printing trade

Printing had spread along the Rhine to Cologne by 1465. New presses were founded by the partners, employees, or fee-paying pupils of the first printing houses. Entrepreneurs in the existing manuscript book trade often provided the capital, markets and management. As printing involved the production of a large number of copies, it required a large investment in paper before a single copy could be sold. The expensive and technically complex equipment of a printing house had to be completed far in advance of any return on capital. This was the trade to which Caxton brought his experience as businessman, diplomat and translator.

We cannot assume that Caxton stood at the composing frame himself or pulled the bar of the press. He may well have learned the techniques of printing but as a wealthy fifty-year-old merchant he had no need to practise them. It was not so much as a craftsman but rather as a capitalist and entrepreneur that he brought the new art first to Bruges and then to England. Caxton's patrons – the Duchess Margaret of Burgundy, Clarence, Edward IV and Henry VII, their queens and children, and the great lords Rivers, Hastings, Arundel, Oxford, the merchants Bryce and Pratt, and other 'divers gentlemen' or 'worshipful persons' subsidized Caxton's books, either by a present of money, or by undertaking to buy a reasonable quantity of them, probably for use as gifts.

Caxton: the first English publisher

Of the 107 separate pieces printed by Caxton seventy-four were books in English. Some twenty of these were in the publisher's own translations; Caxton himself supplied his press with new texts in the vernacular, which no other fifteenth-century printer did except Caxton's associate in Bruges, Colard Mansion. These translations, together with the prologues and epilogues he wrote for his books, secure for Caxton an important place in the development of English prose. The historian G. M. Trevelyan commended Caxton's zeal for the dissemination of books in English: 'His diligence and success as a translator did much to lay the foundation of literary English and to prepare the way for the great triumphs of the following century.'

The other English prose works that Caxton printed were largely translations made by noblemen (Earl Rivers' *Dicts or sayings of the philosophers*, the Earl of Worcester's *Declamation of noblesse*), by Chaucer (*Boethius*), and by others less exalted.

It is to the great credit of Caxton and his 'divers gentlemen and friends' that he brought out the first printed editions of some of the chief glories of mediaeval English literature; the first edition of the *Canterbury Tales* (1478) was followed by a second in 1483, and Caxton's immediate successors brought out further editions. Above all, the printing and publishing of Malory's *Morte d'Arthur* can, in the perspective of 500 years, be seen as Caxton's finest and most enterprising service to English literature.

Caxton often took pains in collating, improving or supplementing the text he printed (as in *Dicts or sayings*, and the *Canterbury Tales*, second edition), in discussing its differences from other authorities (as in the *History of Jason*), and in compiling new material from other sources (as in the *Polycronicon* and the *Golden Legend*).

Caxton's prologues and epilogues

Caxton is one of the few fifteenth-century writers in English who discussed what they were trying to do. Caxton's epilogues and prologues often combine the information of a normal colophon with a dedication and all that a modern editor would put in a preface or postscript. They are in fact little essays on the preceding text, as much part of English literature as of English printing.

Caxton did not hold such importance for his contemporaries that they felt constrained to record the details of his life and work. Much of what we know about him is derived from what he tells us about himself in the prologues and epilogues to the books he printed, written to persuade prospective purchasers that the books were worth buying.

Caxton and Burgundy

In the later fifteenth century the magnificent court of the Dukes of Burgundy enjoyed an unrivalled prestige throughout Europe in matters of culture and fashion. England perhaps more than any other country looked to Burgundy for literary and artistic examples. Caxton, an Englishman long resident in the Burgundian territories, wealthy and well connected, was admirably placed to take advantage of this courtly taste, and to satisfy a prevailing demand with his relatively inexpensive and plentiful printed editions.

The 1467 inventory of the Duke of Burgundy's library is divided into categories which correspond closely to the broad divisions of Caxton's published output; they differ where Caxton printed the chronicles of England instead of those of France and substituted for the 'Livres de Ballades et d'amours' works of the greatest English poets: Chaucer, Lydgate and Gower. They, like Caxton, had worked for noble patrons, basing their poems on fashionable continental models and establishing a 'courtly' style in English.

Caxton and the English language

Caxton, confronted with the different Middle English dialects, had to choose: 'Certainly it is hard to please every man by cause of diversity and change of language,' he wrote. He amusingly illustrated these differences by the anecdote of the Kentish woman whom a London merchant asked for some 'eggs'. 'And the good wife answered that she could speak no French.' It was only when another man asked for 'eyren' (the Kentish plural of 'egg') that 'she said she understood him well'.

By adopting the language of London and the Court in the books that he printed, Caxton did much to fix a permanent standard for written English.

Caxton's reputation as a printer

The eminent American typographer Daniel Berkeley Updike remarked that Caxton would be a commanding figure in the history of English printing even if he had never translated or published a single book: 'He was a great Englishman, and among his many activities, was a printer. But he was not, from a technical point of view, a great printer.' This view has been widely held, partly because Caxton's press-work was sometimes careless; but also because the florid *bâtarde* letter was no longer admired. Nevertheless the *bâtarde* types that Caxton commissioned and used demonstrate to the full the punch-cutter's skill: they simulate well the flow of the Burgundian calligraphy of his day. Caxton evidently went to considerable trouble to reproduce the overall appearance of a page of manuscript text, with its uneven lines and other scribal conventions.

Caxton's types

This is a summary account of the different types Caxton used during his career. The types used for each book are specified in the catalogue entries. Plates illustrating each type are to be found placed near the catalogue entry for the example chosen.

Early printers used for each class of text a type modelled on the manuscript hand in which scribes would normally write such a text. Except in Italy, where the script and type we call roman was particularly favoured, vernacular literature was reproduced in national varieties of the semi-cursive book-hand known as *bâtarde*.

TYPE I

Caxton's first supply of type (type I) was cut and cast by Johann Veldener, a printer and type-founder; first at Cologne, where he probably initiated Caxton into printing. It may have been Caxton who persuaded him to move to Louvain in 1473, where he was well placed to help Caxton. Veldener cut most of Caxton's types, which he also used himself and supplied to other customers. Caxton's type I is modelled on a Burgundian book-hand quite different from the types used by Veldener at Cologne and may have

Type 1. Recuyell of the Histories of Troy, *1474 (13).*

been manufactured in Louvain as part of the job of equipping Caxton's press. Type 1 was perhaps modelled on a hand used by Colard Mansion for his manuscripts.

A *bâtarde* typeface perpetuates distinctively cursive features of its manuscript model: looped ascenders, groups of two or more letters tied in a ligature, sloping long 's' and 'f' with their tails below the line, and contractions.

Caxton ordered an ornate *bâtarde* face for the courtly vernacular texts he wanted to print, an imitation of the book-hand that scribes used for such texts. He wanted too to reproduce the over-all appearance of a luxury manuscript without regard for saving space (and therefore paper) or type; indeed the fount comprises about 160 different sorts, of which twenty-five are combinations of long 's' with other letters.

Both the English books printed by Caxton in Bruges were printed in type 1. Caxton used this type in three other books only, all in French, e.g. the French edition of the *Recueil*. This type is open to criticism in that the individual letters do not always group themselves naturally into words, but it was probably its wastefulness that led Caxton to abandon it altogether and acquire a second type from Veldener.

Type 2. Dicts and Sayings of the Philosophers, *1477 (22).*

TYPE 2

Caxton's second type, first used in Bruges for a French text, *Cordiale*, was taken to equip the new printing house in Westminster, along with his third type, also a design of Veldener's. Caxton continued to use his type 2 for six or seven years, with some modification. It is, like type 1, an imitation of the ornate Flemish book-hand familiar to the Burgundian court and those who shared its literary tastes. The full fount consisted of 217 sorts.

Where type 1 with its broad, rounded, widely spaced letters has a sprawling effect on the page, type 2 has narrower, taller letters and gives texts a more unified and rich appearance. Type 2 was cut and cast by Veldener, and, like type 1, was perhaps based on a manuscript model by Mansion.

TYPE 2*

In February 1479 Caxton discarded the first state of his type 2 for a new casting, type 2*, evidently made by Veldener from the same matrices or punches, but trimmed to produce a more slender outline. There are some new sorts, e.g. in type 2 the letters 'th' are printed from two separate sorts, but in type 2* from a single ligatured sort. The full fount contains 254 sorts.

Wyth the ſemblable Wylle of hym /ought to be put forth
tofore al other thynges . z ther is no thyng ſo reſëblyng
and lyke to the bees that maken hony ſo couenable in
proſperite and in aduerſite as is loue . For by loue
gladly the bees holden them to gyder .   f iij

Type 2* . The Game and Play of Chess, *1482 (49)*.

TYPE 3

Caxton intended to use type 2 for setting vernacular texts. While he was still in Bruges he therefore acquired another type, a gothic, for Latin texts and as a display type for headings. This type 3 has a face larger than type 2, but a body of the same height for convenience in conjunct setting. Veldener was the maker, and Mansion is most likely to have been the designer. Its capitals reveal its Burgundian origins (as several resemble those of type 2). The fount is large: 196 sorts without figures; there are a considerable number of tied sorts, especially combinations of 't' and 'p' with a following letter. Type 3 was probably not complete when Caxton left Bruges because it was first used in significant amounts late in 1478 in the Chaucer Boethius.

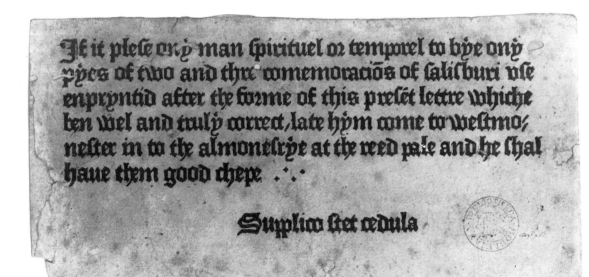

Type 3. Advertisement, 1479(Bodleian Library) (32).

[14]

almyghty God to prouyde yf it be his Wylle . Thenne me semeth
it necessary and expedyent for alle cristen prynces to make peas /
amyte and allpaunce eche With other·and prouyde by theyr Wyse
dōmes·the resistence agayn hym for the defense of our fayth and
moder·holy chirch/ & also for the reuperacion of the holy londe &
holy Cyte of Iherusalem/ In Whiche our blessyd sauyour Ihesu
Crist redemed Vs With his precious blood. And to doo as this no
ble prynce Godeffroy of Boloyne dyde With other noble and hye
prynces in his companye· Thenne for thexhortacion of alle Cristen
prynces /Lordes/ Barons/ Knyghtes /Gentilmen/ Marchauntes/
and all the comyn peple of this noble Royamme Walys & yrelnd
I haue emprysed to translate this book of the conquest of Iheru;

Type 4. Godfrey of Boloyne, 1481 (45).

TYPE 4

Caxton's type 4 was a reduced version of his
type 2, with shorter side-flourishes and with a
few capitals (A, C, D, G, S) resembling his type 3.
With this smaller type Caxton could produce
(and translate) longer books without unduly increasing the expenditure on paper, which made
up about half the total cost of printing. This was
to have a new importance, since, in the latter
part of 1480, Caxton's first rival arrived in
London, John Lettou (the Lett), who had learned
the craft in Rome.

The first dated book in type 4 is the *Chronicles
of England* (10 June 1480). The full fount consists
of 194 sorts, substantially fewer than Type 2*,
Caxton's largest fount.

TYPE 4*

Type 4, after three or four years' use, was due for
replacement; and Caxton needed an increased
supply of type for the production of his long-
planned and most ambitious books, the *Golden
Legend* and the *Morte d'Arthur*. In type 4* the
face-size of type 4 remains unchanged but the
body-height is enlarged to give an agreeable
increase of space between the lines. Type 4* is a
recasting of type 4 with half a dozen matrices
struck from new or altered punches, and some
ligatures omitted. Veldener, then working near
Utrecht, again supplied the new type.

The first dated book in type 4* is Mirk's
Festial (30 June 1483); the fount size was reduced
from 194 to 187 sorts.

also my wytte & Vnderstondyng
Whiche is ryght lytel can not
Vtter ne Wryte thys matere With
oute errour/ Neuertheles Who so
Vnderstondeth Wel the letter/ shal
Wel compryse myn entencyon /
By Whiche he shal fynde nothyng
But moyen for to come to saluac̃;
coon /To the Whyche may fyna
Bly come alle they that Wyllyng;
gly rede/ or here/ or do thys book
to be rede. Amen

Whyche Werke Was fynysshed
in the reducyng of hit in to en ;
glysshe the xviij day of Juyn the
second yere of kynge Rychard
the thyrd /And the yere of our
lord M CCCC lxxxiij / And
enprynted the fyrst day of de ;
cembre the same yere of our lord
& the fyrst yere of kyng Harry
the seuenth/

℄ Explicit p̃ William Caxton

Type 4. Charles, the Great, 1485 (76).*

lastyng lyf in heuen / I purpose to attende by the suffraunce of
almyghty god to tráslate a book late delyuerd to me to reduce
it out of frenſſhe in to our commyn englyſſhe tonge. in whyche
euery man may be enformed how he ouzt to kepe the lawe to
comaũdemẽts of god. to folowe vertu to flee to eſchewe vyces
to to pourueye to ordeyne for hym ſpyrituel rychelles in heuen
ppetuel to permament / Which book was made in frenſſhe atte
requeſte of Phelip le bele kyng of fraũce in the yere of thyncar
nacion of our lord M CC lxxix. to reduced in to englilfhe at

Type 5. The Royal Book, 1487 (79).

ſore / Whiche I knowe not digne ne worthy to treate of ſo
hye matere / ne durſt not only thynke what blame hardynes
cauſeth whan ſhe is folyſſh / I thêne nothyng moeued by ar
rogaũce in folyſſh preſũpcion / But admoneſted of Verray af
feccion to good deſyre of noble men in thoffyce of armes / am
exorted after myne other eſcriptures paſſed / lyke as he that
hath to forn beten doun many ſtröge edyfices / is more hardy

Type 6. Faytes of arms, 1489 (84).

Romanoꝑ Pontificũ Canonice intrācium perſiſtentibꝯ impendere to ſalutarē penitēciã miiungere Ita t
ſepius rõſtitutis abſolucio ipſa impendaf / Nichilominꝯ iterato in vero mortis articulo poſſit impendi
ritate aplica de aplice poteſtatis plenitudine conceſſit facultatem prout in Ipſis litteris aplicis ſuper
Cũ aũt, Magiſter henricus 2ßoſt
Dicti beneplaciti de facultatibꝫ ſuis Competentem quãtitatem ad opus fidei hmoi ac ad repugnacionem
tenore pxlentium hmõi Confeſſoris eligendi et Auctoritate apoſtolica qua In hac parte fungimur fa
ſatiſfaccio impendenda plenam ac liberam tribuimꝯ facultatem / Datum Sub Sigillo Sancte Cruc
oxilleſimo Quadrangēteſimo Octuageſimo Nono Die vireſimo quarto Menſis Aplis

Type 7. Indulgence, 1489 (83).

TYPES 5, 6 AND 7

After the death of Edward IV, Caxton was de-
prived of many of his patrons, and turned to a
wider range of work. First, he needed a new type,
a gothic design, for church Latin texts. Type 5,
cut by Veldener, was a reduced, lighter version of
type 3, and Caxton used it for English books as
well as Latin. It was not until 1488–9 that Caxton
introduced the *bâtarde* type 6 (a reduced version

of type 2) and the small gothic type 7 (a reduced
version of type 5), both probably cut by Veldener
before he went out of business in 1486.

Type 5 was first used in Maydestone's *Directorium Sacerdotum* [1486]; the fount consists of 138
sorts. The first dated book in type 6 is Christine
de Pisan's *Faytes of Arms* (14 July 1489); the fount
has 138 sorts. Only one work in type 7 is known,
the *Indulgence* of 1489; there were only about 100
sorts in the fount.

[16]

that Thomas had made for hym
and praid the kyng that he mygh
te haue it/and he wold gyue hym
asmoche golde as he toke thomas
Thenne the kyng toke his cousey
le & sayd nay/J wyl haue it mysel
fe/Lete hym make the a nother/
for his broder had seen the paleice
in paradyse made with golde/and
arayed wyth precious stones. &
clothe of golde/Thenne the kyng
toke cristendom & many a thou-
sande wyth hym/ and whan the
Bysshop saw that the kynge and
soo moche other peple forsoke her
lawes/and torned to cristendom
they were sore wroth wyth tho-

quomodo sint indiuidencia vna
tres persone/ Primum est qui
a vnum est in homine sapienci
a et de vna procedit intellectus
Memoria et ingeniū:memoria
est vt non obliuiscaris intellec
tū/ vt intelli gas que ostendi
possunt vel doceri.ingenium est
vt quod didiceris iuenias/ Se
cundum est quia in vna vinea
tria sunt lignum folium & fruc
tus/ Et hec omnia tria sunt
vinea / Tercium est quia ca
pud nostrum er quatuor senci
bus constat/ Jn vno autem ca
pite sunt / Visus.Auditus·Ado
ratus. et gustus / Et hec plura
sunt et tamen vnum capud/

Types 6 and 8. Mirk's Festial, *1491 (104).*

TYPE 8

By about 1490, type 5 was worn and due for replacement by type 8, which Caxton obtained not
from the Low Countries but from Paris. It is a
large gothic text and heading type, much used in
Paris from the late 1480's on by Maynyal, the
printer of Caxton's *Sarum Missal*, and by other
printers there. Type 8 is used in only two surviving books, *Ars moriendi* and the second edition of
Mirk's *Festial*, although two of the *Horae* are
known to have been printed in it. Owing to its
superior cut, fewer ligatures were required, and
the full fount was probably not more than 80 sorts.

CATALOGUE

Caxton's birth and education

We have William Caxton's own word for the county, but not the place, where he was born and bred. In the prologue to the first book he printed he tells us: 'I was born and learned mine English in Kent in the Weald'. In the prologue to *Charles the Great* he says: 'I am also bounden to pray for my father's and mother's souls, that in my youth set me to school, by which by the sufferance of God I get my living.' This is all the certain knowledge we have of Caxton's birth and education until his name appears in archival sources, from which it is possible to work out that he was probably born between 1420 and 1424.

Caxton's family

It is probable that William Caxton was a member of a family originating from Cawston in Norfolk towards the end of the thirteenth century, who flourished for 200 years as cloth-traders, mercers, property owners and professional men, with branches in London and Kent. Tenterden, a weaving town in the Kentish Weald, could well be Caxton's birthplace.

King Edward III, noticing (as Fuller remarks in his *Worthies of England*) that 'Englishmen knew no more what to do with their wool than the sheep that wore it', had invited Flemish weavers to settle in Kent in 1331. For the next 400 years Kent was one of the chief areas for the weaving, fulling and dyeing of wool.

Caxton's family was connected with the cloth trade and with the Mercers' Company, the pre-eminent Livery Company in the City of London and. a wealthy fraternity of cloth merchants. Caxton's father, who may have been the elder Thomas Caxton of Tenterden mentioned in certain Tenterden documents, apprenticed William to a Mercer in London. The first documentary evidence for an event in Caxton's life is the entry in the annual Warden's Accounts of the Mercers' Company for the year ending 24 June 1438; it records payment of the enrolment fee of two shillings for his apprenticeship to Robert Large.

1 *Sale by Philip Caxton of the manor of Wratting in Kent, 17 December 1436.*
Add. Charter 75507.

This charter is one of a series of fifteen deeds, all dated between 1420 and 1467, relating to the Caxton family of Little Wratting in Kent. Although it cannot be proved that William Caxton the printer was connected with the Little Wratting family, these charters offer some indications of a possible relationship.

The exhibited charter, written in English, records the sale of the manor of Wratting to John Cristemasse, citizen and draper of London, in 1436. The left-hand seal is that of the vendor, Philip Caxton. Next to it is a damaged impression of the seal of office of the Lord Mayor of London, affixed at Philip Caxton's request 'for as moche as the seal of the said Philip to many folke is unknowen'. The two smaller seals are those of Alderman Robert Large, the Mercer to whom Caxton the printer was shortly afterwards apprenticed, and of Alderman Thomas Cateworthe, acting as witnesses to the transaction.

Robert Large

Caxton's master, Robert Large, was one of the four annual Wardens of the Mercers' Company in 1427, became Sheriff of London in 1430 and in 1439 Lord Mayor. During his apprenticeship to Large, Caxton began to acquire the business experience and personal contacts which were later to be so important to the success of his second career as a printer.

Robert Large made his will on 11 April 1441 and died on 24 April. He left money to his widow (who probably carried on the business), to his sons and to his five apprentices, one of whom was Caxton.

(2) *Caxton's apprenticeship payment. Mercer's Company: Warden's Account Book, 1391–1464.*

Caxton's apprenticeship

2 *Record of payment for Caxton's enrolment as an apprentice, 1437–38.*

Mercers' Company: Wardens' Account Book, 1391–1464, f.128b.

Lent by the Worshipful Company of Mercers.

This entry in the Wardens' Account Book records that in the year between 25 June 1437 and 24 June 1438 Robert Large paid the usual fee of two shillings to the Mercers' Company for the entry of William Caxton into his apprenticeship. Payment of this fee does not necessarily mean that Caxton became Large's apprentice in the same year, as payment was not always made promptly and occasionally was made only shortly before the completion of the apprenticeship. From this record, however, we can arrive at an approximate date for Caxton's birth. If Caxton was apprenticed in 1438 at the youngest possible age (14), he would have been born in 1424. He was still an apprentice in 1441, when he is mentioned in Large's will as such, and if he issued from his apprenticeship then at the maximum age (26), his birth year would have been 1415. The evidence suggests, however, that Caxton was apprenticed in or shortly before 1438 at the normal age of 14–17, in which case his birth year would lie between 1420 and 1424.

The Mercers' Company

The Mercers' Company was one of the most influential of the London guilds; its members were engaged in the wholesale export of woollen cloth. They also dealt in other textiles, including silks and haberdashery, and indeed in many other profitable wares. The Mercers traded chiefly with Flanders and the Low Countries. Outlets in France had been restricted by the Hundred Years' War; the Staple of Calais was reserved for un-woven wool and further east the Hanseatic League endeavoured to keep a monopoly of trade. Although weaving was also the major industry of Flanders, the English cloth trade, producing its own raw materials, could compete favourably with Flemish weavers dependent on imported English wool from Calais on which duties were payable.

It was usual for a promising apprentice Mercer to complete his training overseas, where he would act for his London-based master. Possibly about 1444–5 Caxton went to Bruges, the centre of the Mercers' trade with the Low Countries, where, as he remarked in the prologue to the *Recuyell of the Histories of Troy* (c.1475) 'I have continued by the space of thirty year for the most part in the countries of Brabant, Flanders, Holland and Zeeland'.

Bruges

The Dukes of Burgundy, Philip the Good (1419–67) and then Charles the Bold (1467–77) owed allegiance to the King of France for their French possessions; in practice they behaved as independent princes. The English government during the Hundred Years' War looked to Burgundy for support in retaining or regaining the English territories in France. England also had close trade connections with the Dukes' rich territories in the Low Countries, where Bruges was the main commercial centre.

Bruges was one of the greatest and richest of cities where merchants from all over Europe traded. Among the principal buildings were the Church of St Donatien, where the booksellers and illuminators had their stalls in the cloister; the ducal palace, one of the favourite residences of the Dukes of Burgundy; the public baths; and the Waterhall, a two-storied covered dock and cloth market where barges were unloaded. Here was a great crane, adorned with painted effigies of crane birds, and worked by a tread-mill. Luxury goods could be bought, including fine illuminated manuscripts in the Burgundian taste, and (from the 1460's on) printed books imported down the Rhine.

As in all the great trading centres, each mercantile nation had its communal residence, courts, Governor and charter of privileges.

3 *Record of Caxton's first Livery payment, 1452.*

Mercers' Company, Wardens' Account Book, 1391–1464, f.176b.

(Photograph by courtesy of the Worshipful Company of Mercers)

In the autumn of 1452 Caxton returned to London to take the livery of the Mercers' Company; this entitled him to wear the ceremonial uniform or livery of the Company and to hold office.

The four names at the top of the page are those of the Wardens of the Company for 1452–3. The new livery men of that year paid their £1 fee in three annual instalments; at the side of the first column of names is a note (in French) indicating that the amounts listed were received as livery payments for the first year. Sixteen Mercers each paid 6s. 8d. for the first of their three annual instalments; but in the right-hand column Henry Lytelton paid 20s. outright.

Caxton's name is entered at the bottom of the left-hand column; but his name and Richard Burgh's have been crossed out because, as a note in the margin explains, 'they are among the debtors at the end of the account', where their names are duly listed.

Underneath the livery payments the total revenues from this source are given. Below this are recorded the fines on those who failed to accompany the Lord Mayor, the Mercer Geoffrey Fielding, to Westminster, on 29 October 1452. Each absent Mercer was fined 3s. 4d. and Caxton's name is seventh in the second column.

Caxton the Mercer

In the earliest document concerning Caxton as a freeman Mercer he stood sureties for the debts of an English stapler. Private surety jobbings of this sort were a normal means of credit dealing, a substitute for banking facilities. Caxton was by then evidently in a prosperous way of business.

On 11 December 1453 he signed and sealed a document by which he assigned all his property to Robert Cosyn, another Mercer, and a certain John Rede. This transaction was a legal fiction, possibly conferring a security for credit, or intended to protect Caxton's assets in London or Bruges during his absence from either place.

These and other archival remains reflect Caxton's activity as a Mercer; he shipped woollen cloths from England to Bruges where he sold them. With the proceeds he bought manufactured goods and luxury articles (including books?) at the four great seasonal fairs of the Low Countries (at Bruges, Bergen-op-Zoom, Antwerp and Middelburg) to sell in London. Each deal was usually based on interest-bearing credit, disguised (to avoid the sin of usury) as debts and lawsuits in the records of courts of law or civic authorities.

The Merchant Adventurers

Merchants based north of the Alps and engaged in overseas trade did not depend for their living on their individual capital but pooled their resources in associations such as the German Hanse or the Merchant Adventurers of London, who traded mainly in cloth and whose members were mainly wholesalers.

The English merchants in the Low Countries had been an organized body since the thirteenth century. By Caxton's time the English Nation at Bruges were mostly Mercers and their Governor was usually a Mercer. The controlling Court of Adventurers in London was held in the Mercers' Hall, and its minutes were kept in the same book as those of the Mercers' Company. The Court appointed the Governor at Bruges, the most important and lucrative post open to a Merchant Adventurer.

Caxton: Governor of the English Nation at Bruges

The Middelburg document of 12 August 1462 referring to Caxton as Governor of the English Nation shows that Caxton was certainly then already Governor. In June 1462 his predecessor in office was dismissed, apparently for accepting a bribe. The appointment is a measure of Caxton's wealth and reputation, and possibly also of his Yorkist sympathies. In the Wars of the Roses the Mercers tended to support the Yorkist cause; and Edward IV had only recently gained the English throne.

Caxton's duties as Governor were concerned with the regulation of commerce, arbitration between merchants, dealing with town councils, and upholding the rules of the Merchant Adventurers and the Mercers' Company. He also acted as Edward IV's ambassador in disputes and negotiations with the Dukes of Burgundy and the Hanseatic League.

Caxton the diplomat

Caxton was Governor during difficult times. The commercial treaty governing trade between England and the dominions of the Dukes of Burgundy had fallen into abeyance, although a prolongation of one year had been obtained in October 1461 at Valenciennes. Caxton as Governor became the merchants' representative in negotiations for renewal of the treaty.

On 20 October 1464 Edward IV nominated Caxton as one of his envoys for the trade delegation. A renewal of the agreement was obtained, but was effectually nullified by an edict of Duke Philip's, banning the import of English cloth into his dominions. Caxton as Governor ordered the English merchants to leave Bruges and move out of the Duke's territory to Utrecht, where they held a winter fair early in 1465. The English Parliament retaliated by an embargo on all Burgundian goods except food. Not until the death of Duke Philip in 1467 and the accession of his son Charles the Bold did this deadlock begin to break. In 1468–9 Caxton was kept busy as one of the ambassadors sent to negotiate new terms. In one of his few quiet moments, in March 1469, he began translating the *Recuyell of the Histories of Troy*.

4 Transcript of a letter sent by the Court of Merchant Adventurers to Caxton in Bruges, 4 June 1467.

Mercers' Company: Acts of Court, 1453–1527, f.144b.

(Photograph by courtesy of the Worshipful Company of Mercers)

The Court of Merchant Adventurers, meeting in London on 3 June 1467, received a letter from Caxton dated from Bruges on 26 May; enclosing a copy of a letter to Caxton from the Earl of Warwick concerning the ban imposed by Act of Parliament on imports from the Burgundian dominions.

The Court sent a letter to Caxton as Governor of the English Nation in Bruges instructing him to enforce the provisions of the Act, in accordance with Warwick's letter.

(5) *Record of Caxton's appointment as an ambassador. Mercers' Company: Acts of Court, 1453–1527, f.12.*

5 *Record of Caxton's appointment as an ambassador, 9 September 1468.*

Mercers' Company: Acts of Court, 1453–1527, f.12.

Lent by the Worshipful Company of Mercers.

The manuscript exhibited here, the first volume of the Acts of Court of the Mercers' Company, contains not only the minutes of the Mercers' Company but also those of the Merchant Adventurers from 1453 to 1527. It is a transcript made in a legal hand in the first quarter of the sixteenth century by William Newbold, later Clerk of the Mercers' Company.

The Court of Merchant Adventurers records the appointment of William Redeknape, John Pykeryng and William Caxton as the King's ambassadors 'to go over in Ambassat with divers Enbassators into Flaunders as for the enlargyng of wollen clothe'. This was only one of several occasions on which Caxton served in such a capacity.

Caxton's part in international politics

In November 1467 a treaty was concluded by which a number of privileges were restored to the English merchants, although the ban on English cloth remained. Charles the Bold agreed to take Edward IV's sister, Princess Margaret of York, as his third wife; the English hoped that this marriage would encourage the granting of further concessions, and strengthen the commercial and political links between the two countries.

As a result of the restrictions imposed on English trade and of his own involvement in negotiations, Caxton may have wished to diversify his own business interests. The book trade and the new invention of printing gave him the opportunity to do this. Books were one of the items in which Mercers dealt; Caxton's activity as a publisher and bookseller perhaps represented an expansion of one part of his business.

Margaret of York, Duchess of Burgundy

In April 1467 Duke Charles received in Bruges an embassy which included Caxton, sent to negotiate an end to the trade war and a marriage between Charles and Margaret of York, Edward IV's sister. The marriage (for a huge dowry) and a mercantile treaty to last thirty years were agreed upon, but the ban on English cloth was retained as a bargaining counter even when it was not enforced.

Margaret and Charles were married on 3 July 1468 at Damme, near Bruges. Nine days of festivities followed, which included fireworks, fountains flowing with wine, and sumptuous tournaments and pageants, the gorgeous trappings of obsolete chivalry, in which the nobility and the wealthy delighted.

Caxton and Margaret of York

Margaret of York, born in 1446, was nearly fifteen years old when her eldest surviving brother was crowned King in 1461 and twenty-two when she was married to Charles the Bold.

Caxton had served on diplomatic missions to the court of Burgundy throughout the 1460's and had been head of the English colony at Bruges that welcomed Margaret of York on the occasion of her marriage. Margaret herself, like other members of the Yorkist royal family, engaged in the cloth trade, and Caxton could well have served her as a commercial agent and adviser and was paid a yearly fee. Like Caxton, Margaret was an avid reader of pious literature and chivalric romances; she was also a patroness of scribes and authors. The Duchess gave him encouragement in his work of translating and publishing as well as financial help.

Caxton's association with the Duchess and the splendid Burgundian court recommended his books to the attention of potential customers in England; her patronage was a sufficient guarantee of their being in the 'courtly' style favoured by the English reading public since Chaucer's time.

Moreover, Caxton's first translation, the *Recuyell of the Histories of Troy*, became in 1475 his first production as printer. The provision of multiple copies of an English translation indicates an intention to capture the English home market, as there were not enough Englishmen at the Duchess Margaret's court to create a demand which only printing could satisfy.

Caxton and noble patronage for vernacular books

The fashion of noble patronage for the production of illuminated vernacular texts in a large format, set in France in the fourteenth century by King Charles V and the Duc de Berry, was followed with enthusiasm by the Dukes of Burgundy. Duke Philip the Good and his son, Charles the Bold, Edward IV's ally and brother-in-law, were both notable book collectors, and so was Louis de Gruthuyse, in whose house in Bruges Edward IV stayed in 1470-1. It is to their example that we owe the commissioning and collection of such books by Edward IV, who formed with them the foundations of the Old Royal Library, eventually presented to the British Museum by George II in 1757.

The Flemish illuminators catered for a class who wished to be read to, rather than to read themselves. The volumes they produced were intended to be placed on a lectern and read aloud by a standing lector, over whose shoulder the noble owner could look at the miniatures without inspecting them too closely in detail.

Caxton was denounced by Gibbon for not printing any classical Latin texts. The Dukes of Burgundy, whom the English nobility and Caxton accepted as arbiters of literary taste, favoured books in the vernacular, as can be seen from inventories of their library. Just as the ducal secretaries made translations into French prose for the Dukes of Burgundy, so Caxton made translations into English prose for the English nobles. Caxton may have been acquainted with, and had access to, a major library of vernacular books in Flanders, for which books were constantly being translated from Latin.

6 Jean de Wavrin: *Premier volume des anchiennes et nouvelles chroniques dangleterre.*
Royal MS 15 E. iv.

This manuscript was made in Flanders, perhaps in Bruges, for Edward IV, whose arms appear in the lower border of the right hand page. It probably dates from shortly after his period of exile there in 1470-1. In the exhibited miniature (ff.13b–14) Edward, wearing the Order of the Golden Fleece, is shown receiving the book from its author, who had dedicated it to him. The other figures have been tentatively identified as, on the left, the King's brother Richard of Gloucester (wearing the Garter) and Louis de Gruthuyse, who had been their host in Bruges and, on the right, Lords Rivers and Hastings, who had accompanied them into exile. This volume of Wavrin's chronicle, which is in French, ends with events of the year 1336.

Prologue de lacteur sur la totalle recollation des sept volumes et an
chiennes et nouuelles croniques Dangleterre a la totale loenge du no
ble roy Edouard de [...] He de ce nom. Icta

Edouard par la gra
ce de dieu roy de
france et dangle
terre seigneur dir
lande. Pour ce que au commen

cement de toutes choses contendis
a bonne fin. Selonc la sentence
des philozophes anchiens doit
estre chuse requise a celluy dont
on sa desir mettre en estuat

(6) *Jean de Wavrin presenting his chronicle to Edward IV. Royal MS 14 E. iv, f.14.*

7 *Statutes of the Order of the Golden Fleece.*

Harley MS 6199.

Exhibited is a full-length portrait of Duke Philip the Good (f.57b), who founded the Order in 1429 at the time of his marriage to Isabel of Portugal. The present manuscript records the chapters of the Order up to that of 6 May 1481 and was probably made shortly after this had taken place. The text is in French. Duke Philip was an outstanding patron of artists and writers and the courtly taste which he encouraged was to have a great influence on the choice of texts made by Caxton.

8 *Ordinance of Charles the Bold for the regulation of his military levies.*

Add. MS 36619.

Duke Charles is shown in this miniature (f.5) promulgating the ordinance in the midst of his court. His initial, linked with that of Margaret of York, is included in the decoration of the room in which the ceremony is taking place. The border surrounding the miniature includes the arms of the various territories under Charles' control. The text of the ordinance, which is dated at Trier in 1473, is in French.

9 *Le Dyalogue de la Duchesse de Bourgogne a Iesu Christ.*

Add. MS 7970.

In the frontispiece (f.1b), which is attributed to the Master of Girard de Roussillon, Margaret of York is portrayed kneeling at the feet of the Risen Christ. The manuscript, written and illuminated between 1468 and 1477, contains a devotional treatise in French and is typical of the surviving religious books made in Flanders for Margaret after her marriage to Duke Charles.

Edward IV and the Woodville family

In 1464 the Earl of Warwick, the King-maker, working for an anti-Burgundian alliance, proposed a royal marriage between Edward IV, his protegé and Bona of Savoy, the sister-in-law of Louis XI of France. Edward, however, married secretly Elizabeth Woodville, a widow and a commoner, whose numerous and ambitious family provided him with a ready-made King's party which would free him from dependence on Warwick's power. Edward conferred titles, posts and noble marriages on the Woodvilles.

Thus Elizabeth's father was made Treasurer of England and Earl Rivers in 1466. The rise of the Woodvilles naturally caused resentment and jealousy amongst the older Yorkist nobility. When Warwick rebelled against Edward in 1469 he had the Queen's father, Earl Rivers, beheaded and Anthony, her brother, thus became Earl Rivers. The new Earl accompanied the King on his flight to the Low Countries in 1470. He was evidently a favourite of Edward's, for he was made a Knight of the Garter in 1466 and in 1473 he was appointed governor to the young Prince of Wales. Rivers became a friend and later a patron of Caxton's.

10 Christine de Pisan : *Poems.*

Harley MS 4431.

This magnificent copy of the French poems of Christine de Pisan, written and illuminated in France at the beginning of the fifteenth century, could well have been seen and admired by Caxton himself. One of the names on the flyleaf is that of Earl Rivers, and the book includes Christine's *Dits moraux*, which Caxton printed in a translation by Rivers as *Moral Proverbs* in 1478. The opening of this work is shown (ff.259b–260).

The manuscript was made for presentation by the authoress to Isabel of Bavaria, queen of Charles VI of France. On a flyleaf are the signatures of three distinguished fifteenth-century bibliophiles. The first is Jacquetta of Luxembourg, second wife of John, Duke of Bedford, who probably acquired the manuscript from the French royal library, purchased by her husband when he was regent of France for his nephew, Henry VI. Jacquetta was, by her second marriage, the mother of Earl Rivers. The second is Rivers himself. The third is Louis de Gruthuyse,

(**9**) *Margaret of York kneeling before the Risen Christ. Add. MS 7970, f.1b. (Opposite.)*

host to Edward IV and to his suite, including Rivers, in 1470-1.

Christine de Pisan's voluminous writing enjoyed enormous popularity amongst the nobility of France and Burgundy throughout the fifteenth century. She was the daughter of an Italian scholar and astrologer attached to the court of Charles V of France. Left a widow at the age of about twenty-five, she devoted her life to her pen, supporting her family of three by her writings. Her *ballades* and her *Cité des dames* champion the cause of women and she condemned the *Roman de la Rose* for its attitude to her sex. She also wrote about chivalry.

Edward IV and George, Duke of Clarence

When Warwick the King-maker went over to the Lancastrian party and with Clarence (Edward IV's brother) invaded England, Edward fled to the Netherlands, accompanied by his brother Gloucester (later King Richard III), Rivers and Lord Hastings.

Warwick took Henry VI from the Tower and restored him to the throne. Edward's queen Elizabeth Woodville took sanctuary at Westminster Abbey where she gave birth to her first son.

In 1471 Edward, with the support of Charles the Bold, returned to England and recovered his kingdom at the battles of Barnet and Tewkesbury. It was given out that Henry VI died in the Tower of London 'of pure displeasure and melancholy', but there is no doubt that he was murdered. Clarence, who now realized that his ambitions were thwarted by the terms of Warwick's French alliance, went over to his brother Edward's side. The victorious Edward raised money by issuing pardons and levying fines, which both the guilty and the apprehensive were anxious to accept, among them Caxton on 8 March 1472.

Caxton becomes a printer

Caxton had for nine years served his fellow merchants as a judge and administrator, and the Crown as a diplomat, in the most prominent and lucrative office open to a private Englishman abroad. At some time between the autumn of 1470 and March 1471 he ceased to be Governor of the English Nation, probably in some measure as a result of the temporary Lancastrian restoration in England; by the end of 1472 he had become a printer. The reasons for this change in Caxton's career can only be suggested. It seems likely that it was the eclipse in the fortunes of the Yorkist Mercers and Adventurers that impelled Caxton to make this change, remarkable in a man in late middle age.

He resided for a while, between March and June 1471, at the court of Margaret, Duchess of Burgundy, while, at her request, he worked on his translation of the *Recuyell*. By about the middle of June he had arrived in Cologne and in September he finished his translation of the *Recuyell*. By this time he had probably already turned his mind to printing. Three different printers were then active in Cologne, and one of them became Caxton's master and partner: the anonymous printer of the *Flores Sancti Augustini* (1473). This printer also produced the *De proprietatibus rerum*, the thirteenth-century encyclopaedia by Bartholomaeus Anglicus and it was by taking part in the production of this book that he learned to print.

Johann Veldener

The type used by the printer of the *Flores* was made by Johann Veldener, a native of Würzburg. He later became one of the most distinguished and prolific makers of type in the Low Countries, and Caxton became an important customer of his. Veldener described himself in 1474, after he left Cologne and set up business in Louvain, as a master of his art, skilful 'in cutting, engraving, pressing and stamping, and also in designing and fashioning and whatever in the art is more closely hid'. This means that he was an independent publisher-printer, that his skills included the cutting of punches and casting of type, and that he was competent to teach others. It is very likely that it was Veldener who taught Caxton.

·Despite his semi-retirement and new career as a printer, Caxton continued to play a part in Edward IV's negotiations with the Hanse. He was a member of trade delegations to the Burgundian court, and engaged in the provision of ships for Edward's forthcoming invasion of France ('in conquering his rightful inheritance' as Caxton himself puts it in the dedication of the *Game and Play of Chess*).

The Hanseatic merchants

The Hanseatic merchants in London lived in the Steelyard (where Cannon Street Station now stands) and enjoyed privileges which were not reciprocated, as English traders were excluded from Baltic and German ports. In 1468 Edward IV arrested and fined the Hanseatic merchants, who were then recalled from England. Only one Hanseatic city, Cologne, was allowed to retain its privileges, with sole possession of the Steelyard: Caxton was concerned in the negotiations between the King and the Hanseatic merchants.

11 Entries in the Aliens' Register of the City of Cologne, 1471, 1472, concerning Caxton's residence in Cologne.

(Photographs by courtesy of *Historisches Archiv*, Cologne)

In the Register of Aliens at Cologne are four entries of permission given to William Caxton to reside in the city for successive periods. The first and the last are:

Wednesday 17 July 1471: Wilh. Caxton uyss Engelant ad mensem cum resignatione iij dierum.
Friday 19 June 1472: Wilhem Kaxton uyss Engelant continuatum ut supra ad medium annum cum resignatione uiij dierum.

Caxton came to Cologne on 20 June 1471 and stayed there eighteen months or more, until some date within six months after midsummer 1472.

We know that on 21 March 1472 Caxton took out a royal pardon, possibly to avoid confiscation of property or to defend himself against the threats of enemies. He evidently intended the pardon as a safeguard for his eventual return to Bruges. Caxton's stay in Cologne can be seen as a voluntary and protective exile, although he was probably engaged in confirming Edward IV's exclusive grant of privileges to the Hanseatic merchants of Cologne.

During this period he learned to print and the book he helped to produce was an edition in Latin of the *De Proprietatibus rerum* of Bartholomaeus Anglicus, which is alluded to in Wynkyn de Worde's verses at the end of Trevisa's English translation of this work (*c.*1495):

And also of your charyte call to remembraunce
The soule of William Caxton, the fyrst prynter of this boke
in Laten tongue at Coleyn hymself to avaunce
That every well disposyd man may thereon loke.

(**11**) *Aliens' Register, City of Cologne, 1471–72. First entry for Caxton's residence (line 5) (Historisches Archiv, Cologne).*

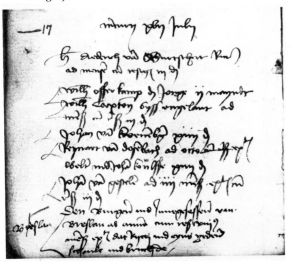

12 Bartholomaeus Anglicus: *De proprietatibus rerum.*
[Printer of the Flores Sancti Augustini: Cologne,
1472.] Duff 39.
IC 3771.

The first book with which Caxton's name is
associated as printer is this Latin edition of the
encyclopaedia compiled by the English Franciscan Bartholomaeus Anglicus. Although written in the thirteenth century, this mediaeval encyclopaedia of human knowledge was still immensely popular, both in England and abroad.

Although this Bartholomaeus has no date or
imprint its type shows that it came from the
press of the anonymous Printer of the *Flores
Sancti Augustini* (possibly to be identified as
Johann Veldener). Caxton's share in the transaction probably included finance: the *De proprietatibus rerum* was a larger book than Veldener
had previously attempted, and Caxton may have
paid for the paper for it.

Caxton and Colard Mansion

Colard Mansion, a copyist and bookseller, appears in the records of Bruges as a supplier of
books to Duke Philip and to Edward IV's friend
Louis de Gruthuyse. In 1472–3 Mansion was
dean of the Guild of St John, the corporation of
booksellers in Bruges. He, like Caxton, sought to
expand his business by making his own translations into the vernacular, and by learning to
print.

Although Caxton and Colard Mansion are not
mentioned together in any surviving document,
their careers were linked, and they were almost
certainly for some years partners in one printing
business. William Blades in 1861 maintained that
it was Mansion who taught Caxton to print.
L. A. Sheppard in 1952 showed that Mansion's
press did not start until at least a year after
Caxton's, and concluded that it was Caxton who
taught Mansion. Wytze and Lotte Hellinga have
argued from Mansion's unusual colophon to his
Jardin de dévotion ('Primum opus impressum per
Colardum Mansion') that this was the first book
Mansion printed in his own name as an inde-

pendent printer-publisher, by contrast with
other books printed anonymously and with
another person. The unnamed associate would
be Caxton and these earlier books the four French
texts printed by Caxton in Bruges.

It is significant that Mansion, like Caxton and
no other contemporary printer, was a translator
who printed his own texts or multiplied them in
manuscript. He too supplied his text with prologues and epilogues, interspersed with personal
observations.

There are telling technical similarities between
the work of the two printers. During the 1470's
the uneven line-endings which many printers
adopted from scribal practice were being replaced by a straight right-hand edge to the type-
page: the newer method is seen in the Bartholomaeus, which Caxton helped to print. But all six
books from Caxton's Bruges press have uneven
line endings which he did not give up until 1480;
and so do Mansion's books up to 1479.

13 Raoul Le Fèvre: *The Recuyell of the Histories of
Troy.* Translation by Caxton finished 19 Septem-
ber 1471.
[Printed at Bruges, probably 1475.] Type 1.
Duff 242. STC 15375.
C.11.c.1 (De Ricci 3:3)

The History of Troy, Caxton's first book, was
translated and printed under the patronage of
Margaret, Duchess of Burgundy, for a noble
clientele among whom stories of the Trojan war
were very popular. Margaret herself personified
the 'new Helen' when she arrived as a bride at
the ducal court in 1468. Caxton wanted to exploit
this market with a translation of the latest 'best-
seller', a French version of these stories, recently
made for the Burgundian court; the first version
in two books only had appeared in 1464, and the
version with a third book still later.

It was in March 1469 at Bruges, Caxton tells
us, that he began to translate the *Recueil des
Histoires de Troye*, a compilation in French prose
made for Duke Philip by his chaplain Raoul Le
Fèvre. After completing 'five or six quires' he
laid the task aside for two years because, he says
with characteristic false modesty, he did not feel

Thus endeth the seconde book of the recule of the histo-
ryes of Troyes/Whiche bookes were late translated in to frensshe out of latyn/by the labour of the vene
rable persone raoul le feure preest as a fore is said/And
by me Indigne and vnworthy translated in to this rude
englissh/by the comandement of my said redoubtid lady
duches of Bourgone : And for as moche as I suppose
the said two bokes ben not had to fore this tyme in oure
englissh langage, therfore I had the better will to accom
plisshe this said werke/ whiche werke was begonne in
Brugis/ and contynued in gaunt And fynysshid in Coleyn
In the tyme of þ troublous worlde/ and of the grete deuy-
sions beyng and reygnyng as well in the royames of
englond and fraunce as in all other places vnyuersally
thurgh the world that is to wete the yere of our lord a
thousand four honderd lxxi . And asfor the thirde book
whiche treteth of the generall and last destruccion of Troye
Hit nedeth not to translate hit in to englissh/ffor as moche as that worshipfull and religyous man dan John lidgate
monke of Burye dide translate hit but late/ after whos
werke I fere to take vpon me that am not worthy to bere
his penner and ynke horne after hym . to medle me in that
werke . But yet for as moche as I am bounde to con-
templaire my sayd ladyes good grace and also that his
werke is in ryme/ And as ferre as I knowe hit is not
had in prose in our tonge/ And also parauenture/ he
translated after some other Auctor than this is/ And
yet for as moche as dyuerce men ben of dyuerce desyres .
Some to rede in Ryme and metre . and some in prose
And also be cause that I haue now good leyzer beyng in
Coleyn And haue none other thynge to do at this tyme

(**13**) Recuyell of the Histories of Troy, *1474.*

sufficiently competent in either English or French. When towards March 1471 Caxton was sent for by the Duchess Margaret at her palace at Ghent 'to speak with her good Grace of diverse matters', she asked to see his incomplete translation of the *Recuyell*. 'When she had seen them she anon found a fault with mine English, which she commanded me to amend, and moreover commanded me straitly to continue and make an end of the residue then not translated.' He completed his task on 19 September 1471.

Caxton had intended to omit the third book of the *Recuyell*, which dealt with the final destruction of Troy, 'for as much as . . . John Lydgate, monk of Bury, did translate it but late, after whose work I fear to take upon me that am not worthy to bear his penner and ink horn after him to meddle me in that work'. (Lydgate's *Troy Book*, a narrative poem written about 1426 is unrelated to the French prose *Recueil*; both works were based on earlier Latin sources.) Nevertheless he translated all the *Recueil*; the Duchess Margaret had ordered the whole, and 'I have good leisure being in Cologne and have none other thing to do at this time'.

Caxton maintained that his qualifications for making such a translation were limited; this disclaimer is a traditional 'humility formula', to be understood by a fifteenth-century reader as intended to commend the book to his indulgence. Similarly Caxton's thirty years' residence abroad is meant to emphasize his imperfect acquaintance with polite English, as is his statement that he was born in the Weald of Kent, well away from London and the Court.

Caxton claimed that he took pleasure in the 'fair language of the French which I never saw to fore like ne none so pleasant ne so well ordered', for the original was written in 'prose so well and compendiously set and written which me thought I understood the sentence and substance of every matter'. When Margaret found fault with Caxton's English it is likely that she thought his style not sufficiently ornate.

The demand for Caxton's English *Recuyell* proved greater than could be supplied by manuscripts. 'And for as much as in the writing of the same my pen is worn, mine hand weary and not steadfast, mine eyes dimmed with overmuch looking on the white paper, and my courage not so prone and ready to labour as it hath been, and that age creepeth on me daily and feebleth all the body, and also that I have promised to diverse gentlemen and to my friends to address to them as hastily as I might this said book, therefore I have practised and learned to my great charge and dispense to ordain this said book in print after the manner and form as ye may here see.' And so towards the end of 1474 or in the first months of 1475 Caxton produced the first book ever printed in English and the first by an English printer, 'not written with pen and ink as other books be, to the end that every man may have them at once, for all the books of this story . . . thus emprinted as ye here see were begun in one day and also finished in one day'. The production of the whole edition, probably of four or five hundred copies, must in fact have taken months; though it is true that every one of the hundreds of copies of each page would be produced within a single day, something obviously not possible by manuscript means.

THE 'RECUYELL' FRONTISPIECE
(Photograph by courtesy of the Huntington Library and Art Gallery, California)

This unique copy of a contemporary engraved frontispiece made for Caxton's first book, the *Recuyell*, shows the Duchess Margaret with ladies-in-waiting, courtiers and a pet monkey; she is accepting a book from a kneeling author, maybe from Caxton himself. This could therefore be the only surviving portrait of Caxton, who looks remarkably young for a man in his mid-fifties.

The engraving is considered to be the work of the artist conjecturally identified by Otto Pächt as the Master of Mary of Burgundy, who made the series of engravings illustrating the Boccaccio, *De casibus virorum illustrium*, printed in 1476 by Colard Mansion. It survives in a copy of the *Recuyell*, now in the Huntington Library, that once belonged to Elizabeth Woodville, Edward IV's Queen.

(**13**) *Engraved frontispiece*, Recuyell of the Histories of Troy, *1474 (Huntington Library)*.

14 Raoul Le Fèvre: *Recueil des Histoires de Troie.*
Royal MS 17 E. ii.

This copy of the *Recueil des Histoires de Troie*, here entitled *Le Livre nommé Hercules*, was written and illuminated in Flanders for Edward IV, probably during the 1470's. The exhibited miniature (f.148) shows Hercules, the principal character of the greater part of the book, slaying the Nemean lion. In accordance with contemporary custom the Valois dukes of Burgundy claimed descent from mythical heroes, including Hercules who was said to have espoused a Burgundian lady named Alise. The royal arms of England appear in the border at the bottom of this page.

15 Jacobus de Cessolis: *The Game and Play of Chess.*
Translation by Caxton.
[Printed at Bruges after 31 March 1475.] Type 1.
Duff 81. STC 4920.
C.10.b.23 (De Ricci 1:1)

Chess was supposed to have been devised as a recreation for kings. The Dominican Jacobus de Cessolis took the game as starting point for a Latin treatise (*c.*1300) on the social classes and the duties of noblemen. The chess-pieces, and their shapes, positions and moves are used as an allegory of human society. He abandons this allegory before the game itself begins, but continues to moralize about social order. Two separate translations into French were made about the mid-fourteenth century, one by Jean de Vignay and the other by Jean Ferron. It is from a conflation of these two that Caxton's English translation was made.

The work was very popular at the Burgundian court; Caxton aimed at a courtly clientele, and so he dedicated it to a suitable sponsor, George, Duke of Clarence, the favourite brother of the Duchess Margaret. 'False, fleeting Clarence', son-in-law, ally and ultimately betrayer of Warwick the King-maker, had designs on his brother's throne – designs at this stage restricted to a claim to be appointed as Edward's chief adviser. Caxton's dedication (modelled on his French original, Jean de Vignay's address to the Prince who in 1350 became King John of France) can be read as discreet propaganda for Clarence and his party as against the Woodvilles.

Caxton makes some personal insertions in the text of the *Game and Play of Chess*. He was involved in a troublesome Chancery suit about this time, and exclaims: 'I suppose that in all Christendom be not so many pleaders, attorneys and men of law as be in England only, for if they were numbered all that belong to the courts of Chancery, King's Bench, Common Pleas, Exchequer, Receipt, and Hell [the record office at Westminster where "dead" documents were kept] and the bagbearers of the same, it should amount to a great multitude. And how all these live, and of whom, if it be uttered and told, it should not be believe.'

Caxton's lawsuit in Chancery of 1475 concerned not debts in the modern sense but a sum due under a credit transaction, and shows that he was then still in business as a merchant.

16 Jacobus de Cessolis: *The Game and Play of Chess.*
French translation by Jean de Vignay.
Royal MS 19 C. xi.

This manuscript contains a collection of moral treatises and poems, most of them French translations of Latin works, beginning with Jean de Vignay's translation of *De ludo scaccorum*. Jean de Vignay (d.1342) was a Hospitaller of the Italian Order of St Jacques de Haut Pas, the chief house of which was in the Rue St Jacques in Paris.

The manuscript was written and illuminated in France early in the fifteenth century. It includes a series of small miniatures in which the various chess-pieces are depicted as persons in different ranks of society. The one shown (f.27b) is the third pawn, a scribe equipped with knife, shears, pen-case and ink-pot at his girdle and with a pen behind his ear.

17 Raoul Le Fèvre: *Le Recueil des Histoires de Troie.*
[Printed at Bruges, 1475.] Type 1. Duff 243.
IB 49410 (De Ricci 3b:1)

Caxton also printed the original French text from which he had made his translation, the *Recuyell of the Histories of Troy*. It was one of the first texts in the French language to be printed.

18 *Cordiale. Les Quatre Dernières Choses.*
[Printed at Bruges, 1476.] Type 2. Duff 108.
IB 49407 (De Ricci 2 : 1)

The *Cordiale* is a treatise on the four last things –
death, judgement, hell and heaven – written in
Latin about 1380–96 by an official of the Order
of Teutonic Knights at Utrecht and translated
into French in 1455 by Duke Philip's secretary,
Jean Miélot.

This work enjoyed a great vogue during
Caxton's lifetime. It appeared in print nearly
fifty times before 1500 in its original Latin, and
there were nearly as many vernacular editions.

Colard Mansion's method of red printing is to
be seen in the *Cordiale*.

This copy from the Old Royal Library is
bound after the *Meditations sur les Sept Psaumes
Pénitentiaux* of Pierre d'Ailly, also printed by
Caxton in Bruges.

Colard Mansion's printing in red

A unique feature of Mansion's work is his unusual method of printing in red. The normal
method was to print the red and black from
separate inkings and impressions. Mansion, however, used to ink the whole page in black, wipe
off the black ink from the appropriate types and
re-ink them in red, and then print off at a single
pull. The results were unsatisfactory, because the
edges of the red ink were tainted by remaining
traces of black, and adjacent areas of black type
were touched with red. (Peter Schoeffer produced the splendid two-colour printing in his
1457 and 1459 Mainz Psalters by a single-pull
method, but he inserted the red type already
inked.) Mansion's method was used on Caxton's
press in the French *Cordiale*, as well as in his own
books.

Caxton's return to England

Caxton had started printing; but he was still involved in the negotiations between Edward IV
and the Hanse and in the King's plans to invade

France in conjunction with Charles the Bold. He
was sent to get ships for Edward in Holland and
Zeeland during April and May 1475.

Edward, however, when help from Charles
was not forthcoming, concluded a separate peace
with Louis XI of France at Picquigny on 29
August 1475 and this brought the alliance
between England and Burgundy to an end.

Caxton, constrained to choose whether to re-
main in business in Bruges or to return to
England, set up as a printer in Westminster in
the autumn of 1476.

Caxton at Westminster

There were many shops in the precincts of
Westminster Abbey and Caxton, from 30 September 1476, paid ten shillings annually as rent
for one of them. The Sacrist's accounts show that
he continued to rent these premises every year
until his death in 1491; and Caxton's assistant and
successor, Wynkyn de Worde, kept the shop on
until his removal in 1500 to Fleet Street. In later
years when this shop was occupied by others engaged in the book trade it was described as
'adjoining the Chapter-house' and 'near the south
door of the church', that is, just to the right of
the Poets' Corner door. The shop was thus con-
veniently sited on a path leading from the royal
palace at Westminster and Westminster Hall to
the Abbey Church and the Chapter-house where
in Caxton's time the House of Commons met.

Caxton also rented two houses and a loft, and
later three houses or tenements in the Almonry,
the site of which is now on the corner of Great
Smith Street and Victoria Street. Here he must
have displayed the heraldic sign of the Red Pale
referred to in his famous Advertisement, although there is no reference to it in the Abbey
records.

19 *Westminster Abbey Sacrist's Roll, 1487–8.*
W.A.M. 19735.
Lent by The Dean and Chapter of Westminster.

On this roll John Estney, the Abbot of Westminster, recorded the receipts and expenditure

(19) *Final entries in Prior Essex's notebook, showing Caxton's payment of a total of 23s. 4d. quarterly for three houses (Westminster Abbey: W.A.M. 33289, ff.26b–27).*

from Michaelmas 1487 to Michaelmas 1488 of the Sacrist's office, which he kept in his own hands. Among his receipts for the rents of tenements within the Abbey precincts occurs (in Latin): 'From William Caxton for the next shop there . . . 10s.' This shop was separated by one which was empty that year from the house called Saint Alban's, rented by the Abbey master mason, Robert Stowell. The shop stood outside the Poets' Corner entrance to the Abbey, close to the Chapter House, and Caxton paid the same rent for it annually from Michaelmas 1476 to the

year from Michaelmas 1491 to Michaelmas 1492 during which (on Caxton's death) it was taken over by Wynkyn de Worde.

The payments for the other premises rented by Caxton at the west end of the Abbey in the Almonry went to the Prior, but his accounts only survive from 1482 until January 1491. It is likely, however, that Caxton's shop in the Almonry at the sign of the 'Red Pale' was the site of his printing press from the time of his return to England in 1476 until his death. A photograph of the final entries for Caxton's payments is shown.

20 *Indulgence.* Single half leaf.
[Printed not after 13 December 1476.]
Types 2 and 3.
Exchequer K. R. Ecclesiastical Documents 6/56.
Lent by the Public Record Office.

The earliest document known to have been printed by Caxton in this country is 'an Indulgence by John, Abbot of Abingdon, a papal nuncio and commissary in England . . . [who] grants, in respect of contributions towards the maintenance of a Christian fleet against the Turks, plenary indulgence of all sins'. The date of issue at Westminster to Henry Langley (who lived at Rickling Hall, Essex) and his wife Katherine is inserted by hand.

The Indulgence is printed on vellum in Caxton's type 2; the abbot's name 'Johannes', apart from its initial letter, was printed in the bold new type 3 for display. In six places the text (in Latin) shows gaps where holes have been nibbled by mice.

Those acquiring this Indulgence were assured of all the benefits they could have obtained by visiting Rome in the previous year, 1475, a year of Jubilee; they were also freed from fulfilling any vows they might rashly have made, except vows to make the pilgrimage to Compostella, to join a religious order, or vows of continence. The other privileges conferred, of choosing one's own confessor and of remission in the hour of death of those sins usually reported to the Holy See, are found in most of the fifteenth-century Indulgences that have come down to us.

The Indulgence was discovered among the Public Records in 1928 by A. W. Pollard, and recognized to be the first recorded piece of printing done in England.

Caxton's 'small stories and pamphlets'

Robert Copland, who worked for Wynkyn de Worde and may even have been apprenticed to Caxton, wrote in the preface to his *Apollonius of Tyre* (1510) that he had translated the work 'according directly to mine author, gladly following the trace of my master Caxton, beginning with small stories and pamphlets and so to other'. This is confirmed by the number of small quartos, a dozen or so, all undated but produced in Caxton's first years at Westminster. The *Disticha* of Dionysius Cato and Lydgate's *The Horse, the Sheep and the Goose*, and *The Churl and the Bird* were among the first of these small books, of which some ran into two or more editions.

21 Raoul Le Fèvre: *The History of Jason.* Translated by Caxton.
[Printed 1477.] Type 2. Duff 245. STC 15383.
C.10.b.3 (De Ricci 64:3)

The *Histoire de Jason* recounts the legend that provided Duke Philip with the theme of his new order of knighthood, the Order of the Golden Fleece, founded in 1429 on the model of the Order of the Garter. Caxton printed this work in French when he was in Bruges and later in his own English translation. Raoul Le Fèvre followed the late mediaeval convention of rewriting a classical legend as if it were a chivalric romance. He presented it to Duke Philip in the 1460's, to glorify the Order of the Golden Fleece.

Caxton in his prologue recalls Duke Philip's remarkable furnishing of the palace at Hesdin in Artois, 'wherein was craftily and curiously depainted the conquest of the Golden Fleece, in which chamber I have been'. The Duke contrived 'in the said chamber by subtle engine that, when he would, it should seem that it lightened and then thunder, snow and rain'.

Edward IV was a knight of the Order of Golden Fleece and *Jason* was a work well suited to bring Caxton's press to the King's notice. Caxton wrote: 'For the honour and worship of our said most redoubted liege lord which hath taken the said Order I have under the shadow of his noble protection enterprised to accomplish this said little book, not presuming to present it to his Highness, forasmuch as I doubt not his good grace hath it in French which he well understandeth . . . I intend by his licence and congee and the supportation of our most redoubted liege lady the Queen to present this said book unto . . . my lord Prince of Wales, our tocoming Sovereign lord, to the end that he may begin to read

(**22**) *Socrates on women.* Dicts and Sayings of the Philosophers, *1477.* (Opposite.)

For I Wote Wel, of What someuer condicion Women ben in
Grece, the Women of this contre ben right good, Wyse, play
sant, humble, discrete, sobre, chast, obedient to their husbon
dis, trewe, secrete, stedfast, euer besy, & neuer ydle, Attemp
rat in spekyng, and vertuous in alle their Werkis, or atte
leste sholde be soo, For Whiche causes so euydent my sayd lord
as I suppose thoughte it Was not of necessite to sette in his
book the saiengis of his Auctor socrates touchyng Women
But for as moche as I had comandemēt of my sayd lord
to correcte and amende Where as I sholde fynde faulte, and
other fynde I none sauf that he hath left out these dictes &
saynges of the Women of Grece, Therfore in accomplisshig
his comandement for as moche as I am not in certayn Whe
der it Was in my lordis coppe or not + or ellis perauenture
that the Wynde had bloWe ouer the leef, at the tyme of trāf
lacion of his booke, I purpose to Wryte the same saynges
of that Greke Socrates, Whiche Wrote of the Women of
grece and nothyng of them of this Royame, Whom I sup
pose he neuer kneWe, For if he had I dar plainly saye that
he Wold haue reserued them inespeciall in his sayd dictes
AlWay not presumyng to put & sette them in my sayd lor
des book, but inthende aparte in the rehersayll of the Werkis
humbly requiryng al them that shal rede this lytyl reher
sayll that yf they fynde ony faulte tarette it to Socrates
and not to me Whiche Wryteth as here after foloWeth

Ocrates sayde That Women ben thapparaylles to
cacche men, but they take none but them that Wil
be poure, or els them that knoWe ben not   And
he sayde that ther isnone so grete empeshment vnto aman

English.' The prince, the future Edward V, born in the sanctuary of Westminster Abbey on 2 November 1470, was then aged six: and Anthony Woodville, Earl Rivers had been appointed his governor to instruct him in 'such noble stories as behoveth a prince to understand and know'.

22 *Dicts or Sayings of the Philosophers*. Translated from the French of Guillaume de Tignonville by Anthony Woodville, Earl Rivers. First edition.
Printed 18 November 1477.
Type 2. Duff 123. STC 6826.
IB 55005 (De Ricci 36:6)

The patron and translator of the *Dicts or Sayings of the Philosophers* was the Queen's brother, Earl Rivers, who on a pilgrimage to St James of Compostella came across the book *Dits des Philosophes*. This was another Burgundian favourite, and Colard Mansion printed it at Bruges soon after Caxton's English edition appeared. The work has its origin in a mid-eleventh century Arabic compilation of sayings attributed to ancient philosophers, which, by way of Spanish and Latin translations, had eventually been translated into French about 1400. Rivers tells us that he 'concluded to translate it into the English tongue, which in my judgement was not before, thinking also full necessary to my said lord the young Prince of Wales the understanding thereof'. In fact there were two earlier English translations, of which both Rivers and Caxton were apparently unaware.

Caxton, when he came to 'oversee his said book and behold . . . how it accordeth with the original being in French', noticed that Rivers had omitted the aspersions of Socrates against women, and he said so. 'I suppose that some fair lady hath desired him to leave it out . . . or else for the very affection, love and goodwill he hath unto all ladies and gentlewomen, he thought that Socrates . . . wrote of women more than the truth.'

'Peradventure', Caxton added, 'that the wind had blow over the leaf at the time of translation'; at the end of his epilogue he himself supplied a version of the missing text. He asked his readers 'if they find any fault to arrest it to Socrates and not to me'. Rivers would not have allowed this addition if it had not shown him in a favourable light as something of a ladies' man. He was an eligible widower, and it had recently been proposed that he should marry Mary, Duchess of Burgundy, the only child of Charles the Bold by his first marriage. (Charles had been killed while besieging Nancy in 1477.) Mary married instead Maximilian, the Emperor's son, in the same year.

23 *Dicts or Sayings of the Philosophers*.
Lambeth Palace Library, MS 265.
Lent by the Archbishop of Canterbury and the Trustees of Lambeth Palace Library.

Earl Rivers commissioned a scribe named Haywarde to write out a copy of his translation for presentation to his brother-in-law, Edward IV. In its dedication miniature (f.ib, shown here) Rivers is seen handing the manuscript to the King, on his throne and with the Queen and the Prince of Wales at his side. The figure kneeling behind Rivers has been identified as the scribe. The manuscript includes both Caxton's colophon and his translation of Socrates' aspersions on women, together with his explanation of Rivers' omission of this passage. The manuscript is dated 24 December 1477, seven weeks after the issue of Caxton's printed edition. Its existence suggests that, although the royal family and the court were offering Caxton extensive patronage and encouragement, they were not prepared to regard a printed book as sufficiently exclusive for a formal presentation of this nature.

24 *Dicts or Sayings of the Philosophers*.
Add. MS 22718.

This manuscript of Earl Rivers' translation, far less elaborate than the one made for the King, was apparently copied from Caxton's second edition of this book, printed about 1480. It belonged to the Hill family of Spaxton in Somerset, and blank leaves at both ends of the volume have been used by them to record births

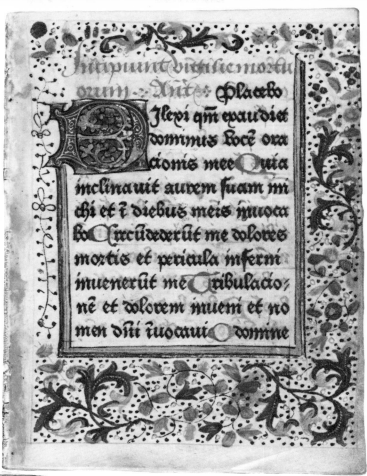

(**25**) Horae, *printed by Caxton c.1476–8, f.1 (Pierpont Morgan Library)*. (Above.)

(**26**) *Book of Hours, illuminated in Bruges, late fifteenth century. Harley MS 2853, f.68b. (Left.)*

and deaths of members of the family and to make notes of useful recipes. The earliest of these additions is dated 1479 and, though this may be a retrospective entry, it suggests that the manuscript came into their possession soon after it had been written. The opening shown (ff.17b–18) has the beginning of the text on the right and some of the Hill family records on the left. This volume serves as a reminder that the introduction of printing did not mean the disappearance of the copy made by hand.

25 *Sarum Horae.* First edition.
[Printed between 1476 and 1478.]
Type 2. Duff 174. STC 15867.
Lent by the Pierpont Morgan Library, New York. (De Ricci 50:1)

This unique fragment represents the first book printed on vellum by an Englishman and is at the same time the earliest liturgical book to be produced by an English printer. It contains the Office of the Dead, of Sarum Use, and the Commendations of Souls, and was once part of a complete Book of Hours. A small fragment of the Hours of the Virgin from the same edition, printed on paper, survives in the Bodleian Library. Caxton printed several later Books of Hours, three known from fragments and two from offsets of their type (see 94), but in no case does sufficient text survive for the Use of the Hours of the Virgin to be identified with certainty. It was, however, almost certainly Sarum, which was virtually standard throughout England.

The Pierpont Morgan fragment is the only English incunable to contain illumination. Its whole appearance is closely modelled upon that of contemporary manuscripts of the Hours, a phenomenon fairly common in Books of Hours printed in the fifteenth century outside England. The blue and red initials in the text, related in form to those belonging to type 2, have been added by hand (microscopic examination suggests that some form of stencil may have been used). The rubric at the top of the exhibited page, together with certain liturgical abbreviations for which type 2 provides no models, are written in by hand with a pen, probably by a professional scribe. It has usually been assumed that this book was printed by Caxton after his removal from Bruges to Westminster. However, he was already using type 2 in Bruges; and both the script of the rubric and the style of the illumination are distinctly Flemish in character. This suggests the possibility that it was printed in Bruges, though it is also possible that the book was illuminated in Flanders or by a Flemish illuminator resident in England.

The fragment of the Hours in the Bodleian Library contains passages from the commemorations of the Saints to be recited at the end of Lauds. These include the Three Kings and St Barbara, both commonly found amongst the miscellaneous devotions in an English Hours but unusual in this particular context. Both were especially venerated at Cologne and it has therefore been suggested that Caxton's first Hours was commissioned by the German merchants of the Steelyard for their private use. This idea, though very attractive, can hardly be regarded as proven.

26 *Book of Hours.*
Harley MS 2853.

This small manuscript Book of Hours is included in the exhibition so that the decoration of its borders may be compared with those in the Pierpont Morgan fragment. The Hours are of Roman Use, and the text is written in a small round liturgical hand often found in late fifteenth-century Flemish manuscripts. The miniatures are by a follower of Guillaume Vrelant, the leading illuminator in Bruges during the third quarter of the fifteenth century, and the style of the borders is close to the style of those found in manuscripts by his own hand. They are typical of the Bruges work of the period.

The manuscript is open to show a miniature of the Nativity (ff.68b–69), introducing Prime.

27 John Russell: *Propositio ad Carolum ducem Burgundiae.*
[Printed probably in 1477.]
Type 2. Duff 367. STC 21458.
IA 55011 (De Ricci 90:2)

This copy of a Latin speech, formerly in the Earl of Leicester's library at Holkham Hall, was purchased by the British Museum in 1951. The only other known copy is in the John Rylands University Library of Manchester. Although without date or imprint, it is plainly the work of Caxton, as it is printed throughout in his type 2; but there is no conclusive evidence to show whether it was printed at Bruges or at Westminster.

It is an undistinguished memorial of a splendid ceremony. Edward IV sought an alliance with Charles the Bold who had succeeded Philip the Good as Duke of Burgundy. Edward's sister Margaret married Charles in July 1468, and Edward admitted him to the Order of the Garter. Among the special envoys charged with the admission and investiture was Dr John Russell, at this time Garter King of Arms. The insignia, which included a golden Garter made by the London goldsmith John Brome, were presented at Ghent with magnificent pageantry; and it was on this occasion that the *Propositio* was delivered by Russell on 4 February 1470.

The *Propositio*, if it was published in Bruges, could not have been printed until the first appearance of type 2 in the French *Cordiale* towards the early summer of 1476 – a long time after Russell made his oration. It is a rare English example of the Latin oration privately printed for the orator for distribution among his friends and prospective patrons. Russell became bishop of Rochester on 6 September 1476; and it is much more probable that the *Propositio* was printed in Westminster early in 1477.

28 Geoffrey Chaucer: *The Canterbury Tales*. First edition.

[Printed 1478.] Type 2. Duff 87. STC 5082.

167.c.26 (De Ricci 22:1); another copy: G.11585 (De Ricci 22:3)

This, the first edition of a great national poem, was not only a considerable printing job (374 leaves) but also required editing. That Caxton later became aware of the problems of establishing a good text we know from the prologue to his second edition of 1483:

I find many of the said books [i.e. manuscripts of the 'Canterbury Tales'] *which writers have abridged it and many things left out, and in some place have set certain verses that he* [Chaucer] *never made nor set in his book, of which books so incorrect was one brought to me six year past, which I supposed had been very true and correct, and according to the same I did do emprint a certain number of them.*

Modern editors divide the manuscripts of the *Canterbury Tales* into two groups according to variations in the order of the tales. Caxton's first manuscript was evidently a text of indifferent quality from Group 'b'; and the manuscript which he used in preparing his second edition was a no better text from Group 'a'.

Caxton brought out six separate editions in all of various poems of Chaucer's, as well as his Boethius translation. He approved too of Chaucer's innovative influence on English:

We ought to give a singular laud unto that noble and great philosopher Geoffrey Chaucer, the which for his ornate writing in our tongue may well have the name of a laureate poet. For to fore that he by his labour embellished, ornated and made fair our English, in this Royaume was had rude speech and incongrue, as yet appeareth by old books, which at this day ought not to have place ne be compared ne to his beauteous volumes.

He comprehended his matters in short, quick and high sentences, eschewing prolixity, casting away the chaff of superfluity, and chewing the picked grain of sentence [i.e. meaning] *uttered by crafty and sugared eloquence.*

Caxton's Chaucer epitaph

Chaucer's tomb in Westminster Abbey was then only a few yards from Caxton's shop. Caxton combined a real enthusiasm for the great English poet with a flair for advertising: he commissioned from an itinerant Italian humanist, Stephanus Surigonus, a Latin epitaph for Chaucer and had it inscribed on a tablet to be hung on a pillar next to the tomb. Caxton also printed it in the epilogue to his edition of Chaucer's Boethius:

Caxton wished you to live after death, illustrious poet Chaucer, through the care of your own William, for he not only printed your works in type, but ordered this praise of you to be placed here.

In 1556 Chaucer's tomb was moved a short distance to its present position, and became the nucleus of Poets' Corner.

29 Boethius: *De consolatione philosophiae.* Translated by Geoffrey Chaucer.
[Printed 1478.] Types 2 and 3. Duff 47. STC 3199.
IB 55018. (De Ricci 8:5)

Boethius (*c.*470–*c.*525 A.D.), a learned Roman, became consul under Theodoric, the Ostrogothic King of Italy, by whom he was later accused of conspiracy and imprisoned. During his long captivity he composed the *Consolation of Philosophy* which became one of the most widely-read books of the Middle Ages. In it Boethius is concerned with finding true happiness in contemplation despite the tribulations of the world.

Between 1475 and 1500 about ninety separate editions of the *Consolation of Philosophy* were printed, most of them in Latin. Among the vernacular editions Caxton's is one of the earliest. At about the same time Colard Mansion published a French version (Bruges, 1477).

Chaucer, says Caxton, was the 'first translator of this said book into English and embellisher in making the said language ornate and fair', and 'the worshipful father and first founder . . . of ornate eloquence in our English'.

In the Boethius Caxton used his gothic type 3 for the first time as intended, i.e. for Latin and for headings; and type 2, superseded early in 1479 by type 2*, makes its last appearance.

30 *Cordiale, or Four Last Things.* Translated from the French by Anthony Woodville, Earl Rivers.
Printed 24 March 1479.
Types 2* and 3. Duff 109. STC 5758.
C.11.c.2. (De Ricci 33:1)

The French translation from the Latin original was printed by Caxton himself before he left Bruges (18), but it was not from this edition that Caxton's friend and patron Anthony Woodville, Earl Rivers, made his English version.

As Rivers' life was taken up in war and politics his choice of a text on the mutability of this world and the certainty of death was entirely appropriate. After the death of his brother-in-law Edward IV, Rivers was arrested and removed on the orders of Richard, Duke of Gloucester (later King Richard III), to Pontefract Castle where he was executed without trial.

Caxton's type 2* here made its first appearance. In the epilogue Caxton mentions that Rivers delivered the manuscript to him on 2 February 1479; he began printing it the next day and on 24 March had finished the total of seventy-eight leaves in fifty-one days.

31 *Cordiale, or Four Last Things.*
Sloane MS 779.

This paper manuscript includes a copy of *Cordiale* transcribed from Caxton's printed edition of the English translation. The copyist has included Caxton's epilogue, the opening words of which appear on the right-hand page of the exhibited opening (ff.150b–151). *Cordiale* is preceded by *The Game and Play of the Chess*, similarly copied from Caxton's printed edition of 1475, at the end of which the scribe records the date of the manuscript as 1484. This volume, like the transcript of *Dicts or Sayings of the Philosophers* (24), indicates that those who required a copy of a specific work were still thinking in terms of a copy made by hand.

'Casting off'

The *Nova rhetorica*, a treatise on the art of Latin speechmaking by the Italian humanist Laurentius de Saona, completed at Cambridge on 26 July 1478, was printed by Caxton in the next year from the author's manuscript, now in the Vatican Library. The manuscript was marked up by Caxton's press editor with marginal figures prescribing the contents of each page in the quires to be printed. This process of 'casting off' was normal in fifteenth-century printing; and necessary when a text had to be divided up for simultaneous printing on several presses, as was Caxton's practice from the *Recuyell* onwards.

Very accurate casting off was necessary for printing 'by the forme', when, in order to conserve type and to enable two or more compositors or presses to work on the same quire, each side of the sheet (containing mostly non-consecutive pages) was set up in type at the same time.

A few other copy texts are known which were similarly marked up and used for printing by Wynkyn de Worde and Pynson in the 1490's.

Photographs are exhibited of MS Vat. lat. 11441, ff.59 and 67b (by courtesy of the Biblioteca Apostolica Vaticana) and of Caxton's edition of the *Nova rhetorica* (by courtesy of Uppsala University Library).

32 *Advertisement*. Single half leaf.

[Printed 1479.] Type 3. Duff 80. STC 4890.

Lent by the Curators of the Bodleian Library (De Ricci 17:1)

The first printed advertisement in English publishing history was this handbill, addressed to 'any man spiritual or temporal' who might wish to acquire 'good cheap' a 'well and truly correct' edition of the Sarum *Ordinal* or *Pye*. It invites customers to come to Caxton's shop, 'to Westminster into the Almonry at the Red Pale'.

The advertised book was 'imprinted after the form of this present letter' i.e. type 3; thus this *Advertisement* constitutes the first English type-specimen, giving potential customers a sample of the type of the *Ordinal*. The direction (in Latin) at the end, 'please leave this poster up', indicates that the *Advertisement* was meant to be affixed to a wall or door: it could thus also be considered as the first English poster.

Only one other copy of the *Advertisement* survives, that in the John Rylands University Library of Manchester; both copies were probably discarded in the printing-house and may have been used to line the same binding.

33 *Ordinale seu Pica ad usum Sarum.*

[Printed 1479.] Type 3. Duff 336. STC 16228.

IB 55007 (De Ricci 82:1)

Of Caxton's edition of the Sarum *Ordinal* or *Pye*, to which the *Advertisement* refers, only these eight leaves have survived. They were discovered in 1858 by William Blades in the damp-mouldered binding of a Caxton Boethius at St Alban's Grammar School. This Boethius binding contained press-waste made up of fragments from thirteen Caxton editions, including two unique copies.

The *Ordinal* was a manual to acquaint the priest with the Office to be recited in accordance with variations in the ecclesiastical year. It was of this manual that the Preface 'Concerning the Service of the Church' in the first Book of Common Prayer observed: 'Moreover the number and hardness of the rules called the Pie and the manifold changings of the service was the cause, that to turn the book only was so hard and intricate a matter, that many times there was more business to find out what should be read, than to read it when it was found out.'

34 *Indulgence*. Single half leaf.

[Printed not after 31 March 1480.] First issue. Type 2*. Duff 204. STC 22582.

IA 55024 (De Ricci 56:1)

This indulgence, printed on vellum, is dated 31 March 1480 and filled in with the names of Simon Mountfort and his wife Emma. Sir Simon Mountfort was beheaded in 1495 along with William Daubeny, a patron and friend of Caxton's (see 76), for complicity with the pretender Perkin Warbeck.

John Kendale, in whose name this indulgence was issued, replaced Abbot Sant of Abingdon as papal commissary. His object was to collect money for the defence of Rhodes against the Turks.

35 *Vocabulary in French and English*. A facsimile edition of Caxton's edition, printed in about 1480, of *Doctrine to learn French and English*. (Duff 405. STC 24865.) With introductions by J. C. T. Oates and L. C. Harmer. Cambridge: at the University Press, 1964.

X 985/4.

In the mid-fourteenth century a schoolmaster living in Bruges compiled for the class-room a *Livre des Mestiers*, i.e. a book of crafts and trades, with French terms and their Flemish equivalents in opposite columns.

Caxton used a later version of it, the conversational manual adapted for the use of merchants and travellers in Flanders in his own day, in order to provide a similar English-French phrase-book. Caxton did not, it seems, translate it himself, as the diction and spelling are quite unlike his. The French text abounds in misprints and sometimes does not make sense. The English too has misprints, and the translations are sometimes inaccurate because they follow a Flemish rather than a French phrase.

A feature of the book is the series of satirical bilingual character-sketches of servants, shopkeepers and craftsmen: 'George the bookseller hath more books than all they of the town. He buyeth them all such as they be, be they stolen or emprinted [the original French must have been '*empruntés*', i.e. borrowed] or otherwise purchased. He hath Doctrinals, Catos [i.e. *Disticha*] Hours of Our Lady, Donatuses, . . . Psalters well illuminated, bound with clasps of silver, books of physic, Seven [penitential] Psalms, calendars, ink and parchment, pens of swans, pens of geese, good Portoses [i.e. Breviaries] which be worth good money'.

36 *The Chronicles of England*. First edition.
Printed 10 June 1480.
Type 4. Duff 97. STC 9991.
IB 55026 (De Ricci 29:8). Printed on vellum.

Requested by 'divers gentlemen' to print a history of England, Caxton turned to the popular *Brut* chronicle. The original of this was the French *Brut d'Engleterre* which followed Geoffrey of Monmouth in naming Brutus, the great-grandson of Aeneas of Troy as the first king of Britain.

The French *Brut* treated the history of England down to 1333; continuations were successively added to English translations to bring them up to date. Caxton's editions of *Chronicles of England* and of Ranulph Higden's *Polycronicon* both in-

clude continuations to the year 1461 which have wrongly been taken as Caxton's own composition. In fact he printed the *Chronicles* from a manuscript of an English translation which already had the continuation; and he reprinted much the same text in the *Polycronicon*.

One entry in the *Chronicles* (for 1457) may have agreeably attracted Caxton's attention:

Also about this time the craft of emprinting was first found in Magonce [Mainz] in Almayne, which craft is multiplied through the world in many places, and books be had great cheap and in great number by cause of the same craft.

In the *Chronicles* Caxton at last abandoned uneven line-endings and justified his lines; he also introduced printed quire signatures for the convenience of binders.

37 Ranulph Higden: *Description of Britain*. (Extract from Trevisa's translation of the *Polycronicon*.)
Printed 18 August 1480.
Type 4. Duff 113. STC 13440a.
C.10.b.24. (De Ricci 35:7)

The *Description of Britain* contains only the geographical sections of Higden's *Polychronicon* which Caxton later printed in its entirety. Nearly all surviving copies are bound with one or other edition of the *Chronicles of England*.

38 *The Metamorphoses of Ovid. Translated by William Caxton, 1480.* Vol. I: the Phillipps manuscript. George Braziller: New York, in association with Magdalene College, Cambridge, 1968. (A facsimile edition.)
MS Facs. 711.

Caxton's prose translation of Ovid's *Metamorphoses* is known only from a two-volume manuscript copy, now in the possession of Magdalene College, Cambridge. The second volume belonged in the seventeenth century to the diarist Samuel Pepys, who left it with his library to the College. The first volume, of which a facsimile is shown, remained unknown until 1966 when it was discovered amongst the residue of the vast collection of Sir Thomas Phillipps, the nineteenth century collector. It was sold in the same year and restored to its companion volume at Magdalene College, partly with money raised by subscribers in England but chiefly through the imagination and generosity of two Americans: George Braziller, who in 1968 published the facsimile edition shown here in order that the proceeds might be devoted to the rescue fund; and Eugene B. Power of University Microfilms, who meanwhile advanced the sum required.

The Ovid text was 'translated and finished by me William Caxton' on 22 April 1480. Whether it was ever printed we do not know. Perhaps Caxton abandoned the project as too costly. Colard Mansion, who printed his splendid French Ovid in 1484, was ruined and had to flee Bruges to escape his creditors. It has been suggested that the Cambridge manuscript could have been written out by Caxton himself for presentation to a patron. However, although we know that Caxton did make a manuscript copy of his earliest translation, the *Recuyell*, before turning to printing as a more convenient method of multiplying his work, the Ovid nevertheless has every appearance of being the work of a professional scribe trained in the Flemish tradition.

The French prose version (*c.*1460) of the *Metamorphoses*, on which Caxton based his translation, re-told Ovid's love tales of gods and mortals, treating them as allegories with moral explanations. It was based in its turn on a late fourteenth-century French verse adaptation of the Latin *Ovidius moralisatus*, composed about 1330 by Petrarch's friend Pierre Bersuire.

The first volume of the manuscript contains four miniatures. The one shown (f.39b) depicts Phaeton tumbling from his chariot and introduces the second book of the text.

39 *Métamorphoses moralisées.* (An allegorized version of Ovid in French prose by Colard Mansion.)
Printed in Bruges by Colard Mansion, May 1484.
IC 49428.

The text is Mansion's own paraphrase of Ovid's poem with moralizations of each episode. The woodcuts are closely related to the miniatures found in Flemish manuscripts of this work, and Mansion's illustrator has successfully transposed his models in terms of block-cutting.

Mansion's fine bold text-type is larger than Caxton's type 2, which it resembles.

Mansion worked as a calligrapher as early as 1450, and probably became Caxton's partner (but not, as was once thought, his master) about 1474. His first dated printed book was Laurent de Premierfait's French version of Boccaccio's *Ruyne des nobles hommes et femmes*, 1476. Although he owned and operated a press on which he printed a score of notable books, Mansion did not cease to produce and sell fine manuscripts for his customers. He left Bruges about June 1484, probably ruined by the expenses of this magnificent book, and is heard of no more thereafter.

40 *The Mirror of the World.* Translated by Caxton. First edition.
[Printed after 8 March 1481.]
Type 2*. Duff 401. STC 24762.
IB 55040 (De Ricci 94:2); another copy: C.10.b.5. (De Ricci 94:7)

This popular account of astronomy, geography and other sciences was written in the thirteenth century and has often been attributed to the Dominican encyclopaedist, Vincent of Beauvais.

Caxton made his translation from a later French prose paraphrase of the French verse *Image du monde* by Gossouin of Metz, and completed it on 8 March 1481. He translated it at the request of Hugh Bryce, an Alderman of the City of London and Keeper of the Mint, for him to present to Lord Hastings, Edward IV's Lord Chamberlain. Hugh Bryce was born in Ireland and became a London goldsmith and alderman. He helped Edward IV to raise the money for Margaret of York's marriage settlement. Edward therefore made a special exception for Bryce when the Parliament of 1478 passed a law by which all Irish-born residents should either return to Ireland, or else pay a special tax for the maintenance of order there.

The woodcuts are the first printed illustrations in any English book; the eleven cuts and eighteen different diagrams are primitive alike in design and execution. Lettering was beyond the engraver's competence, so the explanatory legends were added by hand.

Music.

The spherical world demonstrated.

Arithmetic.

Head of the first chapter.

(**40**) *Woodcuts from* The Mirror of the World, *1481.*

41 *Le Miroir du Monde.*

Royal MS 19 A. ix.

This manuscript contains a copy of the French text from which Caxton made his translation of the *Mirror of the World*. It includes the prologue by the French translator, in which Jean le Clerc of Bruges is named as the patron for whom the text was prepared and the date of its completion is given as 1464. Caxton drew upon information in the French prologue when writing his own, and scholars have believed that he was actually working from the exhibited manuscript. However, Caxton also adds the fact that the French translator finished his work in the month of June, which he cannot have learned from this copy, and his edition has more illustrations than the Royal manuscript.

The manuscript is written on paper and was probably made in Flanders. Diagrams demonstrating the round shape of the earth are shown (ff.43b–44).

English book illustration in the late fifteenth century

Just as the type and layout of the first English printers were often mediocre compared with contemporary work on the continent, so their woodcut illustrations are comparatively crude. There was no native tradition of block-making to guide them, and the English illuminators of the day were producing only shop-work. By contrast the munificent patronage of the Dukes of Burgundy and the Flemish municipalities enabled a succession of painters and illuminators to attain pre-eminence.

When Edward IV in his exile of 1470–2 spent some months in Bruges as the guest of Louis de Gruthuyse, he was so impressed by that great patron's collection that after his restoration he acquired many Flemish manuscripts: a considerable number of these are preserved among the Royal manuscripts in the British Library, and some are included in this exhibition.

Caxton's woodcut illustrations

During the first five years of his career Caxton did not include any illustrations in his books. Of the hundred productions of his press that have come down to us nineteen are illustrated. A great number of the total of 381 woodcuts used in these books were prepared or purchased during the five years 1480–5. They consist of nine series and three miscellaneous blocks. At first Caxton had them cut by English craftsmen, but from c.1486 on he imported blocks already cut on the continent.

In 1481 Caxton published his first two books with woodcut illustrations: the first edition of the *Mirror of the World*, containing a series of woodcuts possibly modelled on the illuminations in a Bruges manuscript; and the third edition of the *Disticha*, in which two of the *Mirror* cuts were re-used. The illustrations in Royal MS 19 A. ix give an idea of the models followed. Caxton employed craftsmen in England who cut woodblocks for him based on pictorial models, printed or hand-drawn.

The second editions of the *Game of Chess* and the *Canterbury Tales* were the next texts which Caxton issued with woodcuts. Their cuts are by a single artist, a different man from the artist of the *Mirror of the World*; this second artist also supplied most of the cuts in *Aesop* and the *Golden Legend*. The later woodcuts take up the full width of a folio page and occupy half its length: a standard size, which was convenient for the compositor setting the text.

42 *The History of Reynard the Fox.* Translated from the Dutch by Caxton. First edition.

[Printed shortly after 6 June 1481.]

Type 2*. Duff 358. STC 20919.

C.11.c.3 (De Ricci 87:1); another copy: G.10545 (De Ricci 87:2)

Caxton finished his translation of *Reynard the Fox* on 6 June 1481. The 'copy which was in Dutch' which he used is now generally identified as the printed edition issued by Gerard Leeu in 1479 at Gouda, though it may have been a manuscript closely related to the one used by Leeu.

Reynard the Fox is a satire, intended (in the words of the Dutch preface) to expose 'the subtle deceits that daily be used in the world'. Caxton adds a solemn joke: 'If anything be said or written herein that may grieve or displease any man, blame not me, but the fox, for they be his words and not mine.'

The lasting popularity in various languages of the story is attested by the adoption in English of Bruin and Tib as the proper names for a bear and a cat, and in French by the replacement of 'goupil' by 'renard' as the common noun for fox.

At the end of quire 'h' the compositor by mistake omitted a page of text and was obliged to insert an extra leaf containing the text of half a page on each side. Both the previous page and the inserted leaf finished with 'for'; and so the compositor missed out one of the pages thus marked up in the 'casting off'.

43 Marcus Tullius Cicero: *Of Old Age* (an anonymous translation) and *Of Friendship* (translated by John Tiptoft, Earl of Worcester); with Bonaccursius de Montemagno's *Of Nobility* (translated by Tiptoft).
Printed 12 August 1481.
Types 2* and 3. Duff 103. STC 5293.
C.10.b.6. (De Ricci 31:3); another copy: C.21.d.29. (De Ricci 31:5)

The anonymous English version of Cicero's *De senectute* (*Of Old Age*) was published in one volume with *Of Friendship* and the *Declamation of Noblesse*, both translated directly from the Latin by John Tiptoft, Earl of Worcester. *Of Old Age* was a translation made from the French version of Laurent de Premierfait to the order of Sir John Fastolf (1378–1459). Although Caxton was a bookseller, the manuscripts he used for his printed editions were not always readily accessible. Of this one he tell us it was 'with great instance, labour and cost comen into my hand'.

Cicero at the age of 63, disillusioned and in retirement from public life, wrote his essay on old age shortly before he was murdered at the instigation of Octavius in 44 B.C. 'Philosophy', wrote Cicero, 'can never be praised as much as she deserves, since she enables a man who is obedient to her precepts to pass every season of life free from worry.'

John Tiptoft, Earl of Worcester, was a distinguished humanist; his Latin eloquence brought tears to the eyes of Pope Pius II. He was also a politician, the merciless 'Butcher of England', who, it was said, 'used the law of Padua not the law of England', before he was himself eventually executed in 1470. Caxton's unexpected praise of the hated Tiptoft can be read as propaganda for Earl Rivers; their careers have certain parallels.

44 Marcus Tullius Cicero: *Le Livre de vieulesse.* Translated by Laurent de Premierfait.
Harley MS 4329.

This richly decorated little manuscript was written in April 1460 for Jean le Gous, secretary of Charles VII of France, by Pierre Le Fèvre. The illumination was executed in the studio of Jean Fouquet, the greatest French painter of the day. The end of Premierfait's prologue and the opening of his translation (ff.32b–33) are shown. The manuscript also contains his translation of the *De amicitia*.

Laurent de Premierfait (d.1418) made a number of French translations from Latin works, including the *De casibus virorum illustrium* of Boccaccio. He was for many years a member of the household of the royal treasurer, Jean de Chanteprime, and enjoyed the patronage of members of the royal family. His translation of Cicero's *De senectute* was made in 1405 for Louis de Bourbon.

Sir John Fastolf, for whom the English translation of the *De senectute* printed by Caxton was originally made, was a notable patron of the arts and of scholarship. After Agincourt he served with the English army of occupation in France, and he died the year before this manuscript was written. One anonymous French illuminator who executed commissions for him and for John, Duke of Bedford, is now known as the 'Fastolf Master'.

almyghty God, to prouyde yf it be his Wylle . Thenne me semeth
it necessary and expedyent for alle cristen prynces to make peas ,
amyte and allyaunce ecche With other, and prouyde by theyr Wyse
dōmes, the resistence agayn hym for the defense of our fayth and
moder, holy chirch, & also for the reuperacion of the holy londe &
holy Cyte of Iherusalem, In Whiche our blessyd sauyour Ihesu
Crist redemed vs With his precious blood. And to doo as this no
ble prynce Godeffroy of boloyne dyde With other noble and hye
prynces in his companye, Thenne for thexhortacion of alle Cristen
prynces, Lordes, Barons, knyghtes, Gentilmen, Marchauntes,
and all the comyn peple of this noble Royamme Walys & yrlond
I haue empryfed to tranflate this book of the conqueft of Iheru-
falem out of ffrenssh in to our maternal tongue, to thentente ten-
courage them by the redyng and heeryng of the merueyllous hif-
toryes herin compryfed, and of the holy myracles shewyd, that e -
uery man in his partye endeuoyre theym vnto the resistence a fore
fayd, And reuperacion of the fayd holy londe, & for as moche as I
knoWe no Cristen kynge better prouyd in Armes: and, for Whom
god hath sheWed more grace, And in alle his empryses gloryous
vaynquysshour, happy and euious, than is our naturel, laWful,
and fouerayn lord and mooft cristen kynge, EdWard by the grace
of god kynge of englond and of ffraunce and lord of yrlond, Vn
der the shadoWe of Whos noble protection, I haue achyeued this
fymple tranflacion, that he of his mooft noble grace Wold, adresse
styre . or commaunde somme noble Capytayn of his subgettes to
empryse this Warre agayn the fayd turke & hethen peple, to Whiche
I can thynke that euery man Wyll put hand, to in theyr propre
perfones, and in theyr meuable goodes, Thenne to hym my mooft
drad naturel and fouerayn lord I adresse this fymple and rude
booke befechyng his mooft bountruous and haboundaunt grace to
receyue it of me his indigne and humble subgette William Caxton, And to pardonne me so presumynge, befechyng almyghty god
that this fayd book may encourage, moeue, and enflamme the her
tes of somme noble men, that by the same the mefcreauntes maye
be resisted, and putte to rebuke, Cristen fayth encreaced, and en -
haunced, and the holy lande, With the blessyd cyte of Iherusalem,
recouerd, and may come agayn in to cristen mens hondes, Thenne
I exhorte alle noble men of hye courage to see this booke and here
it redde, By Which ye shal see What Wayes Were taken: What noble
proWesses and valyaunces Were achyeuyd, by the noble compa-

45 *Godfrey of Boloyne, or The Siege and Conquest of Jerusalem, or Eracles.* Translated by Caxton.

Printed 20 November 1481.

Type 4. Duff 164. STC 13175.

C.11.c.4. (De Ricci 46:4)

Caxton translated *Godfrey of Boloyne* from a French version of the Latin history of the First Crusade of the eleventh century, written by William, Archbishop of Tyre, some seventy years after the conquest of Jerusalem.

Godfrey of Boloyne, the conqueror of Jerusalem, was one of the heroes known as the Nine Worthies: they were three ancients (Hector, Alexander and Caesar), three Hebrews (Joshua, David and Judas Maccabaeus) and three Christians (King Arthur, Charlemagne and Godfrey). Caxton's prologue to *Godfrey* is, among other things, a programme for his forthcoming publications, in which he gives notice of his edition of the story of King Arthur.

Caxton's appeal to Edward IV to lead another Crusade, this time against the Turks (who had recently captured Rhodes and invaded southern Italy), could not fail to please a number of highly placed men, including Earl Rivers and the Indulgence commissaries.

46 Ranulph Higden: *Polycronicon.* Translated by John Trevisa.

[Printed after 2 July and before 20 November 1482.] Type 4. Duff 172. STC 13438.

IB 55060 (De Ricci 49:26)

Higden, a Benedictine monk of Chester (d.1364) composed his universal history, the *Polycronicon* in the 1320's. More than a hundred manuscripts of it are extant. The translator, John Trevisa (1326–1412), was vicar of Berkeley in Gloucestershire. A number of continuations were added to Higden's text in the course of the fourteenth century; and the account of English history in Caxton's edition is extended down to Edward IV's reign; this continuation is taken mostly from that in the *Chronicles of England.*

Caxton considered that Trevisa's verion, although made within ten years of Chaucer's Boethius translation, needed modernizing; he

therefore 'changed the rude and old English, . . . certain words which in these days be neither used ne understanden'.

This vast volume of 450 leaves was on sale no later than 20 November 1482, when a copy was bought from Caxton by a certain William Purde, who noted the fact in the book, referring to Caxton as the 'King's Printer' (*Regius Impressor*).

The copy exhibited is from the Old Royal Library.

47 Ranulph Higden: *Polycronicon.* Translated by John Trevisa.

Add. MS 24194.

Trevisa completed his translation of the *Polycronicon* in April 1387. The work was undertaken for his patron, Thomas, Lord Berkeley, for whom he made a number of other translations. Amongst the prefatory material which he added to the book is a dialogue on the subject of translation between a lord and a clerk.

This copy of Trevisa's translation of the *Polycronicon*, written and illuminated early in the fifteenth century, is of special interest because it bears the arms of Richard Beauchamp, Earl of Warwick (d.1439). Beauchamp's first wife, Elizabeth, was the daughter and heiress of Thomas, Lord Berkeley, patron of Trevisa. On the left side of the opening shown (ff.35b–36) is the last part of a chronological list of events covered by the book, on the right the preface begins with a miniature of the translator at work. This miniature is in the style associated with the studio of Herman Scheerre.

48 Dionysius Cato: *Disticha.* Third edition. Translation by Benedict Burgh.

[Printed 1482.]

Types 2 and 3*. Duff 78. STC 4852.

IB 55034 (De Ricci 15:1)

Caxton published in 1477–8 two quarto editions of the original Latin text of this work; a third edition, in folio, is shown here. It is a late classical collection of moral couplets in hexameters attributed to a non-existent ancient moralist Dionysius Cato. Caxton's editions of the Latin

in the cytees thenne they make good alyaunces ·
And otherwhile they deceyue theyr souereyns whan they
may do hit couertly / For there is no thyng at this day
that so moche greueth rome and Italie as doth the college
of notaryes and aduocates publique / for they ben not of
one accorde. Alas and in Engelond what hurte doon the
aduocates men of lawe and attorneyes of court to the co=
myn peple of the royame as wel in the spirituel lawe as
in the temporalle · how torne they the lawe and statutes
at their plesure / how ete they the peple / how enpoueze they
the comynte / I suppose that in alle cristendom are not so
many pletars attorneys and men of the lawe as ben in
englond onely · for yf they were nombrid alle that longe
to the courtes of the chaunserye + kynges benche + comyn
place + chekez / resayt / and helle / and the bagge berars of
the same · hit shold amounte to a grete multitude · And
how al thyse lyue and of whom / yf hit shold be uttrid and
tolde / hit shold not be beleuyd for they entende to theyr syn
guler wele and prouffyt and not to the comyn / how wel
they ought to be of good wyl to gyder · And admoneste &
warne the cytees eche in his right in suche wyse that they
myght haue pees and loue one wyth another + & Tullyus
saith that frendshyp and good wylle that one ought to
haue ayenst another for the wele of hym that he loueth ·
wyth the semblable wylle of hym / ought to be put forth
tofore al other thynges · & ther is no thyng so resemblyng
and lyke to the bees that maken hony so couenable in
prosperite and in aduersite as is loue · For by loue
gladly the bees holden them to gyder ·   f iij

(49) The Game and Play of Chess, *1482*.

King Evilmerodach 'a jolly man without justice', feeding his father to the vultures.

The philosopher Philemetor.

King Evilmerodach and Philemetor playing chess.

The Smith

Chapter-head: 'Of keepers of towns, customers and toll gatherers'.

The Tailor

(**49**) *Woodcuts from* The Game and Play of Chess, *1482.*

were accompanied by an English verse translation by Benedict Burgh. Burgh, in his youth a collaborator of Lydgate, was a canon of St Stephen's chapel in the Palace of Westminster just over the way from Caxton's shop.

The *Disticha*, used as a school-book throughout the Middle Ages, was often printed by the earliest presses. From this book schoolboys learned Latin and at the same time, it was hoped, sound morals. Caxton in the dedication to his fourth edition described it 'as in my judgement . . . the best book for to be taught to young children in school, and also to people of every age it is full convenient if it be well understanden'. In it he used two woodcuts of a schoolmaster and boys which first appeared in the *Mirror of the World*.

49 Jacobus de Cessolis: *The Game and Play of Chess.* Second edition.

[Printed 1482.] Type 4*. Duff 82. STC 4921.

C.10.b.1. (De Ricci 18:8)

The Game and Play of Chess retained its popularity; in this second and illustrated edition Caxton tells how he first read and translated the book 'at such time as I was resident at Bruges' and then 'did do [i.e. cause to be] set in emprint a certain number of them which anon were depeshed [despatched] and sold'. This is Caxton's only statement of the fact that he printed at Bruges; none of his Bruges books give the place of printing.

The manuscript models for the vigorous series of woodcuts in the *Game of Chess* were probably to be found in some continental manuscript, possibly the same one that Caxton had used in making his translation nearly ten years earlier. Professor N. F. Blake has suggested that as there were not many pictorial models available for the books Caxton wanted to publish, ready access to such models may have been a decisive factor in his reissues of the *Game of Chess* and even the *Canterbury Tales*. In this second edition of *Game of Chess* there are twenty-four illustrations, one for each chapter, but only sixteen separate cuts. The same cut is used to illustrate the chess piece

and, later in the book, its move. The chessboard appears three times.

There is also a revised prologue, as the Duke of Clarence, to whom the first edition was dedicated, had been imprisoned in the Tower in 1477 on a charge of treason, and there drowned in a butt of malmsey. Caxton draws his readers' attention to the woodcuts, in those days still a novelty, especially in England.

As we have seen, a text was 'cast off', i.e. marked up in page lengths before the compositor started work. This process was simplified if the woodcuts, which had to be fitted on the page with the text, were of a standard size, and placed immediately after the chapter headings, or as near to them as possible. Although the text of the last page of a chapter sometimes did not fill the whole page, Caxton's imported paper was expensive and this was an important consideration in his layout.

Caxton had not yet started to use woodblocks for the initial capitals and so these were to be added later by hand, together with the paragraph marks. The compositor therefore left a gap, usually two lines deep, in which the letter to be added was printed in lower case type as a guide to the rubricator.

50 *Psalterium cum canticis.*

[Printed 1482 or 1483.]

Type 3. Duff 354. STC 16253.

IA 55038 (De Ricci 84:1)

This is the only known copy of Caxton's Latin Psalter and may have belonged to Queen Mary Tudor. The rose watermark found in signature i also appears, in a later state, in Normandy documents dated 1484; this suggests the later date, but the signature may have been a cancel, and the rest of the book, on paper with a different watermark printed in 1482.

51 *Curia sapientiae*. ('The Court of Sapience', formerly attributed to John Lydgate.)

[Printed 1483.] Type 4. Duff 260. STC 17015.

IB 55055 (De Ricci 68:3)

An anonymous dream allegory in verse of a controversy between Mercy, Truth, Justice and Peace, the daughters of a great king, followed by a tour through the Palace of Wisdom. The poem, left anonymous by Caxton but later misascribed to Lydgate, was probably composed about 1475 as a compliment to Edward IV and four of his daughters.

King Richard III

Edward IV died unexpectedly on 9 April 1483 aged nearly forty-one. The Prince of Wales, aged twelve, then at Ludlow with his uncle and guardian Earl Rivers, was proclaimed King Edward V. But Edward IV's brother, Richard, Duke of Gloucester, arrested Rivers on 30 April and seized custody of the young King and, later, the King's young brother, the Duke of York. Rivers was executed at Pontefract Castle on 25 June 1483. Richard revived the old scandal that Edward IV was a bastard, and maintained that the new king was a bastard too because Edward IV's marriage to Elizabeth Woodville was bigamous and invalid. The little Princes, Edward V and his brother died or were murdered in the Tower; Richard was crowned king on 6 July 1473 in Westminster Abbey, not far from Caxton's Chapter House shop. The Woodville party was in disarray, and Caxton lost his patrons and friends at court. Edward's Queen Elizabeth Woodville remained invulnerable but imprisoned in sanctuary in Westminster Abbey.

Richard had destroyed the normal succession to the throne. Henry Tudor, through his mother Margaret Beaufort a great-great-grandson of Edward III's son John of Gaunt, was the most powerful claimant; the widowed Queen Elizabeth Woodville promised her daughter Princess Elizabeth in marriage to Henry if he became King. Caxton's publication of the *Knight of the Tower* can be linked with this dynastic manoeuvre.

Caxton and other printers in England

Among the Acts of Richard III's first Parliament was a statute against foreign merchants and craftsmen; there was however an exception made, apparently at the request of the King or his Council, for the import and sale of 'books written or printed', and for the residence in England of merchants and craftsmen engaged in the book trade. This was of benefit to Caxton and to his competitors who were more or less dependent on workmen from abroad.

Caxton's relationship with the other printers in England was one of co-operation rather than rivalry. Theodoric Rood in Oxford, and John Lettou and William de Machlinia in London, rarely encroached on Caxton's chosen field of books in English; they specialized in Latin theology and school-texts, and De Machlinia also printed law texts such as the *Statutes* and *Year Books*. Likewise the Saint Albans Schoolmaster-printer printed mainly school texts and theology.

The presses in London and St Albans used types similar to Caxton's types 2, 3 and 4, presumably supplied by Veldener with Caxton's help; Rood in his last book (1486) used cuts perhaps supplied by Caxton. This year also saw the end not only of the Oxford press but of the St Albans Schoolmaster-printer and of William de Machlinia. During the last five years of his life Caxton remained the only printer in England.

52 *Pilgrimage of the soul.* Anonymous translation of Guillaume de Deguilleville, *Pèlerinage de l'âme.*
Printed 6 June 1483.
Type 4. Duff 267. STC 6473.
IB 55069 (De Ricci 73:1)

During the eleven weeks' reign of Edward V Caxton produced only one book, the *Pilgrimage of the Soul*. It is an anonymous English prose version of a French poem written about 1330 by the Cistercian monk Guillaume de Deguilleville. This English version has been erroneously ascribed to John Lydgate (who did in fact translate a companion piece by Deguilleville, *Pilgrimage of the Life of Man*). G. D. Painter explains the mistake thus: in one copy of Caxton's *Pilgrimage of the Soul* (formerly in the Harleian collection, now in the Yale University Library) a quire of Caxton's edition of Lydgate's *Life of Our Lady* was in error substituted for the right quire. This led the Harleian cataloguer to suggest 'some likelihood that the translation was made by Lydgate'; and others copied this attribution.

53 John Mirk: *Festial (Liber festivalis)*. First edition.
Printed 30 June 1483.
Type 4*. Duff 298. STC 17957 (1).
C.11.c.5.(1). (De Ricci 79:1)

John Mirk was Prior of the Abbey of Augustinian Canons at Lilleshall in Shropshire in the early fifteenth century. His *Festial* is a collection of anecdotal sermons for parish priests, arranged according to the feast days of the Church's year.

The text of Caxton's first printed edition is incomplete, but merely insofar as it was set up from a recension which omitted the author's preamble and colophon. His second edition, however, was set up from the edition printed at Oxford in 1486 and gives a complete text. Prof. N. F. Blake suggests that Caxton sometimes printed what he had to hand in the stock of manuscript books in his shop. Unusually, and perhaps deliberately, Caxton omitted the regnal year in his colophon date; he may have felt the political future too uncertain to risk it.

54 John Gower: *Confessio amantis*.
Printed 2 September '1493' (i.e. 1483).
Types 4 and 4*. Duff 166. STC 12142.
C.21.d.1. (De Ricci 48:1)

In his edition of the *Confessio amantis*, a collection of love stories in verse by Chaucer's contemporary John Gower, Caxton finally gave the regnal year of Richard III. According to N. F. Blake, Caxton's text does not belong to any of the three families in which the surviving manuscripts are now grouped; he probably used a now lost manuscript in which the three recensions were already conflated.

This is one of Caxton's biggest books; this and the *Golden Legend* are his only books on large paper. Gower's short lines enabled him to save paper by printing for the first time in two columns. The *Confessio amantis* is unusual among fifteenth-century books in that the first four-fifths are printed in one type (4), the rest in another (4*). The changeover occurs in quire Z. The first compositor began in the middle sheet of the quire, but after he had set all these four pages in type 4, except the second column of the first page, his colleague setting for one of the other presses took over and set the remaining column in type 4*.

55 John Gower: *Confessio amantis*.
Egerton MS 1991.

The *Confessio amantis*, Gower's only long poem in English, contains stories drawn from Ovid and from other later sources. Successive versions were dedicated to Richard II (d.1400) and to Henry IV, and the book attained immediate popularity in court circles. The manuscript shown is witness to this: it was probably made within the lifetime of the author (Gower died in 1408) and is a fine example of a *de luxe* library book of the period. Only a wealthy man could aspire to own a book of this quality; a number of similar manuscripts survive, each including a copy of the miniature of the lover and his confessor (f.7b). The miniature is in the style of Herman Scheerre, an immigrant from the Lower Rhineland, who had become the foremost illuminator in England at the beginning of the fifteenth century.

Caxton's undated editions, 1483–84

Caxton produced a group of undated books at this period; as they are in type 4* they must be later than June 1483, and from the absence of printed initials and paragraph marks (first used at the beginning of the year 1484) they are assigned by G. D. Painter to the months between July and December 1483. The books are Alain Chartier's *Curial*; Chaucer's *Canterbury Tales* (second edition), *Book of Fame*, and *Troilus and Criseyde*; Lydgate's *Life of Our Lady*; and the *Sex epistolae*.

56 Alain Chartier: *The Curial*. Translated by Caxton.

[Printed 1483.] Type 4*. Duff 84. STC 5057. C.10.b.17. (De Ricci 20:1)

The theme of contempt for a courtier's life enjoyed great favour with a group of scholars towards the end of the fourteenth century. The *Curial*, a folio pamphlet of six leaves is 'the copy of a letter which Master Alain Chartier wrote to his brother which desired to come dwell in court, in which he rehearseth many miseries and wretchedness therein used, for to advise him not to enter into it . . . which copy was delivered to me by a noble and virtuous Earl, at whose instance and request I have reduced it into English.' The Earl was Rivers, recently beheaded. Chartier wrote in Latin; Caxton used the French version of an unknown translator.

57 Geoffrey Chaucer: *The Canterbury Tales*. Second edition, with woodcut illustrations.

[Printed 1483.] Types 4*, 2*. Duff 88. STC 5083. G.11586. (De Ricci 23:3); another copy: IB 55095 (De Ricci 23:2)

For the revised text of his second edition of the *Canterbury Tales* Caxton used a manuscript supplied by a dissatisfied customer. The first edition, printed from 'an incorrect book brought to me six years past' (possibly by a patron, as a commission) had been 'sold to many and divers gentlemen, of whom one gentleman came to me and said that this book was not according in many places unto the book that Geoffrey Chaucer had made. To whom I answered that I had made it according to my copy, and by me was nothing added ne minished. Then he said he knew a book which his father had and much loved, that was very true and according unto his own [i.e. Chaucer's] first book by him made, and said more if I would emprint it again he would get me the same book for a copy, how be it he wist well, that his father would not gladly part from it'. Caxton agreed to print a second revised edition, 'for to satisfy the author, whereas to fore by ignorance I erred in hurting and defaming his book in divers places', and maybe to oblige the gentleman. 'And he full gently gat of his father the said book, and delivered it to me by which I have corrected my book.'

Collations of the text of Caxton's two editions of the *Canterbury Tales* have confirmed what Caxton himself says: that he did not set up his second edition directly from the gentleman's manuscript ('by which I have corrected my book'). He wrote in the corrections, additions and deletions in a copy of his first edition, and printed from that. The work was done in some haste; in one of the copies shown (IB 55095) on f.8 recto there are visible impressions of the 'furniture', quoins and wooden frame that surrounded the type. It was quicker and cheaper for the compositors to set up type from printed text than from a bulky and probably quite valuable manuscript. Also, in casting off a text of this length, it was obviously much easier to judge from 'copy' already printed just how much text would fit on each page; and there was no need to make any marks on the borrowed manuscript.

Caxton was not an editor in the modern sense. He did not suspect that his first text was not the best available until the gentleman pointed it out. He agreed to print a second edition from another manuscript before he had even seen it. He was of course anxious to bring out a second edition of a work for which there was likely to be a demand. Although in Caxton's day some printers did employ scholars to establish good texts of classical authors, this was rarely if ever done with vernacular literature. Moreover, contemporary scholars often tended to be stronger on emendations of their own devising, however good, than on accurate collation of the available manuscripts. Caxton's main consideration was, understandably, practical and commercial: he did not go out of his way to obtain a good text, but did what he could with the manuscripts that came his way.

(**57**) *Prologue:* Canterbury Tales, *1483*. (Opposite.)

[58]

Whan that Apryll wyth hys shouris sote
The droughte of marche hath percyd the rote
And bathyd every veyne in suche lycour
Of whyche vertue engendryd is the flour
Whanne Zephirus eke wyth hys sote breth
Enspyrid hath in every holte and heth
The tendyr croppis / and the yonge sonne
Hath in the ram half hys cours y ronne
And smale foulis make melodye
That sleppyn al nyght wyth opyn eye
So prykyth hem nature in her corages
Than longyn folk to gon on pylgremages
And palmers to seeke straunge strondis
To serue halolwys couthe in sondry londis
And specyally fro every shyris ende
Of engelond to Cauntirbury thy wende
The holy blysful martir for to seke
That them hath holpyn when they were seke

Byfyl in that seson on a day
In Suthwerk atte tabard as I lay
Redy to wendyn on my pylgremage
To Cauntirbury wyth deuout corage
That nyght was come in to that hostelrye
Wel nyne and tbenty in a companye
Of sondry folk by auenture y falle
In feleshyp and pylgrymys were they alle
That tolbard Cauntirbury wolden ryde
The chambrys and the stablys were wyde
And wel were we esid atte beste
And shortly whan the sonne was at reste
So had I spokyn wyth hem euerychon
That I was of her feleshyp anon
And made forwardys erly for to ryse
To take our wey there as I you deuyse
But nathelees whyles I haue tyme and space
Or that I ferthyr in thys tale pace
Me thynketh it accordaunt to reson
To telle you al the condicion

a iij

The Wife of Bath.

The Squire

The Pardoner.

The Pilgrims at supper.

(57) *Woodcuts from* Canterbury Tales, *1483.*

THE WOODCUTS

The twenty-six woodcuts in the second edition of the *Canterbury Tales* depict each pilgrim on horse-back and carrying a rosary: one shows the assembled pilgrims at supper round a table. Some of the cuts are re-used several times, e.g. the cut at the head of the Merchant's Tale is used also in the General Prologue for the Franklin and the Summoner, and at the head of the Summoner's Tale.

The woodcuts were made by the same craftsman who made the blocks for the *Game and Play of Chess*, second edition (1482). The Squire, with curled locks and holding a flower, is the most accurately realized of the Pilgrims. It is puzzling to find the Clerk of Oxenford bearing bow and arrows; and the Miller a slight boyish figure playing not a bag-pipe but a flute.

Wynkyn de Worde inherited Caxton's blocks and used most of them in his 1498 edition of the *Canterbury Tales*. From Wynkyn de Worde the blocks passed to Thomas Godfrey and thirteen of the cuts appear in Godfrey's 1532 edition.

Pynson had the series copied for his first book, the edition of the *Canterbury Tales* he brought out in about 1492. Caxton's twenty-three designs re-appear in this edition surrounded by black borders. The drawing is improved, and there are minor additions: the Miller gets a mill.

Pynson's 1526 edition contains eighteen cuts, including seven not at all improved recuttings. These second copies for no apparent reason follow Caxton's earlier designs rather than Wynkyn de Worde's; an additional block, a new Franklin, derives from Caxton's Manciple, who has no cut of his own in Pynson's first edition of the *Tales*.

58 *The Ellesmere Chaucer. Reproduced in facsimile.* 2 vols. Manchester: the University Press, 1911.

MS Facs. 158.

About eighty manuscript copies of Chaucer's *Canterbury Tales* are known, some of them surviving only in fragments. The most celebrated of them is the Ellesmere Chaucer, so-called after the family that owned it from the seventeenth century until 1917, when it was sold to the Henry Huntington Library and Art Gallery in California. The Ellesmere Chaucer was written and illuminated at the beginning of the fifteenth century. The exhibited book is a photo-lithographic facsimile in which decoration has been substantially redrawn by hand, which accounts for the slightly modern appearance of the figures.

The decoration of the Ellesmere Chaucer is unusually elaborate by comparison with that of other manuscripts of the *Tales*, and includes a mounted figure of each of the Pilgrims at the beginning of his or her Tale. On the exhibited page (f.157b) is the figure of Chaucer himself. This bears a striking resemblance to the marginal portrait of the poet in Harley MS 4866 (on exhibition in the Manuscripts Saloon) and is probably a true likeness. Only two other surviving manuscripts of the *Canterbury Tales* contain mounted figures of the Pilgrims and these are not directly related either to each other or to the Ellesmere manuscript. The woodcut illustrations in Caxton's second edition of the work may have been based upon drawings in a manuscript now lost, but they may equally well have been a completely independent creation.

59 Geoffrey Chaucer: *The Canterbury Tales.*

Harley MS 7333.

A copy of the *Canterbury Tales* is among the miscellaneous secular English literature collected together in this manuscript. Works by Gower, Hoccleve and Lydgate are also included, and the manuscript opens with a copy of the *Brut*. The manuscript was begun about the middle of the fifteenth century and was written out over a period of many years by at least six, and probably nine or more, different hands.

Part of the *Knight's Tale* is shown (ff.45b–46). On the inner margin of the left-hand page is a small drawing, in red ink, of a 'stock' in a 'tun'. This is thought to be a rebus, or pictorial pun, on the name Stockton or Stoughton, and may refer to the scribe of this part of the book. Others of the scribes have left clues to their identity and it is possible that they were all connected with the Augustinian Abbey of St Mary in Pratis at Leicester. A collection of popular secular literature such as this could very well have been made for a religious house, though its contents would be equally suited to a layman's private library. The manuscript has no decoration other than occasional red and blue initials such as appear on the exhibited opening, though rather more ambitious initials mark major divisions of the text. The general appearance of this copy of the *Tales* may be contrasted with that of the much more elaborate and less typical Ellesmere Chaucer.

60 Geoffrey Chaucer: *The Book of Fame* (i.e. *House of Fame.*)

[Printed 1483.] Type 4*. Duff 86. STC 5087.

C.10.b.13. (De Ricci 21:1)

Caxton's name printed in the margin marks the point where the text of Chaucer's never completed dream-poem broke off in Caxton's defective manuscript. Caxton supplied a makeshift 12-line conclusion with a closing couplet:

Thus in dreaming and in game
Endeth this little book of Fame.

Caxton went on to praise Chaucer: 'In all his works he excelleth in my opinion all other writers in our English, for he writeth no void words but all his matter is full of high and quick sentence . . . For of him all other have borrowed since and taken in all their well saying and writing.'

61 Geoffrey Chaucer: *Troilus and Criseyde.*

[Printed 1483.] Type 4*. Duff 94. STC 5094.

C.11.c.10. (De Ricci 26:2); another copy: G 11589. (De Ricci 26:3)

Caxton's printer's copy was a manuscript, now lost, of Chaucer's revised version, in which some leaves were missing and others misplaced. Caxton's edition still remains an impressive first printing of a great poem.

In these two copies of *Troilus and Criseyde* there are two different settings of the outer sheet of quire m, distinguishable by the numerous different spellings used by the two compositors, e.g. in the first line of m1 recto 'herte' and 'hert'. Variant sheets like this are probably reprints made because Caxton underestimated the number of sheets he would require to make up his edition.

The second copy belonged to Lady Jane Grey, to whom it may have descended from her great-great-grandmother, Queen Elizabeth Woodville.

62 John Lydgate: *The Life of Our Lady.*
[Printed 1483.] Type 4*. Duff 266. STC 17023.
C.10.b.18. (De Ricci 71:2)

A poem of 6000 lines on the life of the Blessed Virgin from the time of her marriage up to the Presentation of Christ in the Temple.

63 John Lydgate: *The Life of Our Lady.*
Harley MS 629.

Lydgate's English poem on the life of the Virgin Mary was extremely popular and a considerable number of manuscript copies of it are in existence. Lydgate, a monk of Bury St Edmunds who died about 1457, acted as court poet for much of his long life. His works include a number of devotional poems and verse lives of several saints, amongst them the patron of his own abbey, the martyred King Edmund.

The *Life of Our Lady* was composed at the request of King Henry V. The exhibited copy was made about the middle of the fifteenth century and is unusual amongst manuscripts of this text in having some illumination. The beginning of the prologue is shown (ff.4b–5), opening with a decorated initial typical of the style prevalent in England for much of the century. Proper names are underlined in red.

64 *Sex epistolae.* A correspondence between Pope Sixtus IV and Giovanni Mocenigo, Doge of Venice, about the war of Ferrara, edited by Petrus Carmelianus.
[Printed after 14 February 1483.]
Types 4* and 3. Duff 371. STC 22588.
IA 55067 (De Ricci 92:1)

This exchange of letters, ostensibly a model of humanist Latinity, is in fact a Venetian 'White Paper', with a preface arguing the Venetian case in the matter of the war. It was probably published to influence the English government in Venice's favour. Carmelianus, an itinerant Italian humanist, worked in 1484–5 as an editor for the Oxford printer Theodoric Rood, and eventually became Latin secretary to Henry VII.

This is the only known copy.

65 Geoffroi de la Tour Landry: *The Knight of the Tower.* Translated by Caxton.
Printed 31 January 1484.
Types 4 and 4*. Duff 241. STC 15296.
C.11.c.6. (De Ricci 63:1); another copy:
IB 55085. (De Ricci 63:2)

Caxton's translation of the book 'which the Knight of the Tower made [in 1371–2] for the enseignement and teaching of his daughters' was completed on 1 June 1483 and printed 'the last day of January, the first year of King Richard the third', i.e. 1484. It seems likely from the arrangement of chapters and from verbal details that Caxton made his translation from one of two manuscripts now in the Bibliothèque royale in Brussels, and formerly in the library of the Dukes of Burgundy. The 'noble lady' who had the manuscript passed on to Caxton for translation was probably Queen Elizabeth Woodville, Edward IV's widow and the mother of five daughters; Caxton does not name her because of the political changes since her commission.

The knight wrote in the sensational tradition of late mediaeval sermons, and his stories are often ribald or cruel. Indeed, in Fitzherbert's *Book of Husbandry* (1534), in a section on the duties of wives, the author fears that he will be like the Knight of the Tower, who in his book 'hath made both the men and the women to know more vices, subtlety and craft than ever

The poure ought not to compare hym self to hym whiche is ryche and myghty / As sayth this fable of a frogge / Whiche was in a medowe / Where she aspyed and sawe an oxe whiche pastured / She wold make her self as grete and as myghty as the oxe / and by her grete pryde she beganne to swelle ageynste the oxe / And demaunded of his children yf she was not as grete as the oxe and as myghty / And theyr children answerd and sayd / nay moder / For to loke and behold on the oxe / it semeth of yow to be nothynge / And thenne the frogge beganne more to swelle / ⁋ And when the oxe sawe her pryde / he thradde and thrested her with his fote / and brake her bely / Therfore hit is not good to the poure to compare hym self to the ryche / Wherfore men sayn comynly / Swelle not thy self / to thende that thow breste not

⁋ Here fynysshed the second booke of Esope /
⁋ And after begynneth the regystre or table of the thyrd book of Esope

(**67**) *The frog and the ox, Aesop,* Fables, *1484.*

they should have known if the book had not been made'. To familiar tales from other collections the Knight added anecdotes from his own youth or about people he knew. Caxton shortens or omits passages criticizing the fashions of the Knight's day or dealing with matters of purely local interest.

In the *Knight of the Tower* the first six quires are in type 4 and the last five in type 4*.

66 Dionysius Cato: *Disticha*. Translation by Caxton finished 23 December 1483.
[Printed probably about February 1484.]
Types 2 and 4*. Duff 79. STC 4853.
C.10.b.8. (De Ricci 16:1)

Caxton translated his fourth edition of the Cato *Disticha* from a text in which the Latin original was accompanied by a French prose rendering and commentary. This edition was dedicated to the City of London; but Caxton's attitude to the City is highly critical: 'I have known it in my young age much more wealthy prosperous and richer than it is at this day, and the cause is that there is almost none that intendeth to the common weal but only every man for his singular profit'. Caxton issued his new edition of the *Disticha*, 'by cause I see that the children that be born within the said City increase and profit not like the fathers and olders'. Caxton regrets this: 'But fairer nor wiser nor better bespoken children in their youth be nowhere than there be in London, but at their full ripening there is no kernel, nor good corn founden, but chaff for the most part'.

The raven and the fox.

The two rats.

The jay and the peacocks.

(67) *Woodcuts from Aesop Fables, 1484.*

The author.

67 Aesop: *The book of the subtle histories and fables of Aesop*. Translation by Caxton completed 1483.
Printed 26 March 1484.
Types 3 and 4*. Duff 4. STC 175.
IB 55088 (De Ricci 4:2)

A fable is a short account of an incident or conversation in which animals speak and act like human beings. The story makes a didactic or satirical point – a moral, and the animals provide simplified types of human motive and character.

Aesop was traditionally said to have been a slave in Greece who won his freedom through his skill as a teller of fables. He did not write them down; but gradually collections of fables were compiled and their authorship was attributed to Aesop. The main sources are the Latin verse collection by Phaedrus (*c.*40 A.D.) and others in Latin and Greek, including the 'Life of Aesop'. As Caxton the publisher realized, fables are perennially popular.

About 150 different editions of Aesop's fables appeared in print before 1500, in various languages. Caxton made his translation from the French version of Julien Macho, possibly from the first printed edition published at Lyons in 1480. Macho's text was itself a translation of Heinrich Steinhowel's German-Latin collection printed by Johann Zainer in Ulm, *c.*1476.

For his 186 woodcut illustrations, Caxton's artist copied a celebrated series of designs first made for the Aesop printed by Johann Zainer at Ulm about 1476–7, a series several times re-used by other printers.

The earliest printed collection of Aesop's fables was Ulrich Boner's *Der Edelstein* (printed by Albrecht Pfister, Bamberg, 1461); it was also the first dated illustrated book to be printed. For Steinhowel's collection (Ulm, *c.*1476) Johann Zainer's craftsman reworked designs from *Der Edelstein* and from other manuscript drawings to produce 163 illustrations of the fables, twenty-eight of Aesop's life, a frontispiece and depiction of the author writing. With slight changes the original Ulm cuts reappeared in Augsburg editions: those in the Augsburg edition printed by Gunther Zainer (1477) were the source for the series of cuts in the Lyons edition; the designs

were traced, and some reversed. Caxton's craftsmen chose to redraw rather than trace the French woodcuts, probably so as to eliminate detail and thus keep the cutting within his scope.

The woodcuts in Caxton's Aesop begin with a full-page frontispiece showing Aesop surrounded by symbols from his fables; his gesture is that of a sage expounding an argument. The designs of the fable illustrations are often clumsy; the workmanship is somewhat better and the woodblocks were, with one or two exceptions, cleanly cut.

68 Ramon Lull: *The Book of the Order of Chivalry*.
[Printed about April 1484.]
Types 4* and 3. Duff 58. STC 3326.
IA 55071. (De Ricci 81:1)

Caxton translated his undated *Order of Chivalry* from a French version of the original Catalan of Ramon Lull (1235–1315), the philosopher, knight, mystic and missionary. This treatise on the duties and symbolism of knighthood is, in Lull's fictional setting, given by an old hermit to a young squire seeking to become a knight, who presents it at court to the King.

In his epilogue Caxton says that he translated the book 'at the request of a gentle and noble esquire, according to the copy that the said squire delivered to me'. The squire could well have been Anthony Woodville, Earl Rivers, who at his last tournament in 1478 appeared 'horsed and armed in the habit of a white hermit'. Now that Rivers was dead Caxton presented his book to the new King, Richard III, in honour of the new Prince of Wales, possibly at the instigation of Rivers' sister, Queen Elizabeth, who at this stage wanted a rapprochement with Richard.

The Mercer Caxton shared the aristocratic taste of the Burgundian court, and of Edward IV, for make-believe chivalry and tournaments. He asks Richard to offer prizes for the victors in tournaments and to command 'this book to be had and read . . . that the noble order of chivalry be hereafter better used and honoured'. He addresses the knights of England: 'What do ye now but go to the bains [baths] and play at dice? Alas, what do ye but sleep and take ease?' Caxton the publisher urges them to 'leave this . . . and read the noble volumes of Saint Graal, of Lance-lot, of Galahad, of Tristram, of Perceforest, of Percival, of Gawain and many more. There shall ye see manhood, courtesy and gentleness.'

69 *Le liure de lordre de cheuallerie.*

Royal MS 14 E. ii.

Caxton's translation of the *Order of Chivalry* was made from the French version of Ramon Lull's work. The manuscript copy exhibited, opening with a miniature of the squire instructed by the old hermit, is the fifth and last item in a volume of collected French verse and prose works, written and illuminated in Flanders for Edward IV between 1473 and 1483 (f.338).

70 Jacobus de Voragine: *The Golden Legend*. Translated by Caxton. First edition.

[Printed after 20 November 1483, probably in 1484.] Types 3 and 4*. Duff 408. STC 24873. C.11.d.8. (De Ricci 98:2)

The Golden Legend, the longest of Caxton's books, was printed on large paper: this enabled him to print about 600,000 words in double columns on 448 leaves. It was Caxton's intention to publish, as a companion to the *Polycronicon*, the secular universal history, the sacred *Golden Legend*, the most popular and famous collection of lives of saints. The compiler of the Latin original, the *Legenda aurea*, was Jacobus de Voragine, Archbishop of Genoa in the thirteenth century; he was a Dominican and therefore a preacher, with narrative as well as a didactic talent. No other work of its kind attained a wider currency both before and after the invention of printing than *The Golden Legend*; so called 'because like as gold passeth in value all other metals', Caxton says, 'so this legend exceedeth all other books'. The saints' lives are arranged in order of their feast days.

For his English version of *The Golden Legend* Caxton used Jean de Vignay's French version as his main source, but translated five lives omitted by Vignay direct from the Latin original. He added twenty lives of English saints from the existing English version of about 1430 called *Gilte Legende*, which presumably remained un-known to him until his own translation from the French was completed. Caxton used a Vignay manuscript in which narratives from the life of Christ have been put into a separate section; to this he himself added a companion series of lives from the Old Testament.

Caxton added information and comment to the text of his translation. *The Golden Legend* records that on one occasion when Saint Augustine was preaching the local inhabitants pelted him with fish-tails. As a result 'the children that were born after in that place had tails, as it is said, till they had repented them'. Caxton continues: 'It is commonly said that this fell at Strood in Kent, but blessed be God, at this day there is no such deformity.'

In his prologue Caxton tells us that at one time he despaired of ever completing the translation and printing of this vast work. He was encouraged, however, by the practical help of William, Earl of Arundel, who promised 'to buy a reasonable quantity of them', and also offered Caxton by way of reward a buck every summer and a doe every winter for the rest of his life. Caxton completed his translation on 20 November 1483.

Caxton illustrated his edition with nearly seventy woodcuts, including nineteen large ones occupying the width of a page: these are Biblical and other scenes; and one displays the badge and motto of his patron Arundel. Fifty-one smaller cuts, set in to the two columns of the text, depict the saints with their emblems. These woodcuts are the work of the cutter of the *Game and Play of Chess* illustrations, supplemented by another hand.

71 *Legenda sanctorum in Englysshe.*

Add. MS 35298.

This is one of the most complete and comprehensive copies of the English version of the *Legenda aurea*. It demonstrates the kind of variation between sources which led Caxton to draw on more than one original when compiling his own translation. The three lives of English Saints represented on the opening shown (ff.52b–53) – of St Edward the Confessor, St Winifred of Shrewsbury, and St Erkenwald of London – are all peculiar to this particular manuscript.

(**70**) *The Saints in Glory*. The Golden Legend, *1484*.

The martyrdom of St Thomas à Becket (above), *and the Annunciation* (below).

The Nativity (above) *and the Epiphany* (below).

(**70**) *Woodcuts from* The Golden Legend, *1484.*

Now leue we these knyghtes prysoners and speke we
of syre Launcelott du lake that lyeth vnder the Appyl Tree slepynge / euen aboute the noone there come
by hym foure quenes of grete estate / And for the hete sholdn
not nyke hem there roue foure knyghtes aboute hem / and bare a
clothe of grene sylke on foure sperys betwixe them and the
sonne / And the quenes roue on foure whyte mules

¶ Thus as they roue they herde by them a grete hors grymly
neye / thenne were they ware of a slepynge knyghte that laye
alle armed vnder an appyl tree / anone as these quenes loked
on his face / they knewe it was syre launcelot / Thenne they by-
ganne for to stryue for that knyghte / euerychone sayd they
wolde haue hym to her loue / ¶ We shalle not stryue sayd Mor
gan le fay that was kynge Arthurs syster / I shalle putte an
enchauntement vpon hym / that he shalle not awake in syxe
oures / And thenne I wylle lede hym away vnto my castel /
And whanne he is surely within my holde / I shalle take the
enchauntement from hym / And thenne lete hym chese whyche
of vs he wylle haue vnto peramour / ¶ Soo thys enchauntement was caste vpon syre Launcelott / And thenne they leyd
hym vpon his shelde / and bare hym soo an horsbacke betwixt
two knyghtes / and brought hym vnto the castel charyot / and
there they leyd hym in a chambyr colde / and att nyghte they
sente vnto hym a fayre damoysel with his souper redy dyght
By that the enchauntement was past / And whan she came
she saleweed hym / and asked hym what chere / I can not saye
fayre damoysel said syre Launcelot / for I wote not how I cam
in to this castel / but it be by an enchauntement / Syre sayd she
ye must make good chere / And yf ye be suche a knyght as it is
sayd ye ben / I shalle telle you more to morne by pryme of the
daye / Gramercy fayre damoysel sayd syre Launcelot of your
good wyl I requyre yow / And soo she departed / And there
he laye alle that nyght withoute comforte of ony body

¶ And on the morne erly came these foure quenes passyng-
ly wel bysene / Alle they byddyng hym good morne / and he
them agayne / ¶ Syre knyghte the foure quenes sayd thow
must vnderstande thou arte our prysoner / and we here knowe
the wel that thou arte syre Launcelot du laake / kynge Bans

The Morte d'Arthur

The *Morte d'Arthur* is the most famous version and the first in English prose of 'the matter of Britain': the legends which grew up about King Arthur, and the literature which they inspired.

Why does Caxton's colophon give the title of Malory's work as *Le Morte d'Arthur*, a title which is suitable only for the end, i.e. Books 20 and 21? The text of the manuscript Caxton was using finished: 'Here is the end of the whole book of King Arthur and of his noble knights of the round table . . . and here is the end of the death of Arthur.' Caxton added: 'Thus endeth this noble and joyous book entitled le Morte d'Arthur', and went on, 'notwithstanding it treateth of the birth, life and acts of the said King Arthur, of his noble knights of the round table, their marvellous enquests and adventures, th'achieving of the Sangreal and th'end the dolorous death and departing out of this world of them all'. Mr Paul Needham has suggested that Caxton understood 'the death of Arthur' to be the title of 'the whole book of King Arthur and of his noble knights'. Believing that Malory's original text was French, Caxton gave it a French title, adding this fuller statement of the book's contents.

72 Sir Thomas Malory: *Le Morte d'Arthur*.
Printed 31 July 1485.
Type 4*. Duff 283. STC 801.
(De Ricci 76:1)
Lent by the Pierpont Morgan Library, New York.

Of all the books Caxton printed, only two continue to be widely read: Chaucer's *Canterbury Tales*, and Malory's *Morte d'Arthur*. The *Canterbury Tales* were already esteemed as the greatest poem in English. This is probably what impelled him to print them; as we have seen, the *Canterbury Tales* were preserved in dozens of manuscripts and the text we read now owes little or nothing to Caxton. The *Morte d'Arthur*, however, completed in 1469 or early 1470, was a recent work, and to Caxton goes the credit of editing, printing and publishing one of the greatest books of his day. Until well into the twentieth century Caxton's edition was the only known text. Caxton's publication of the *Morte d'Arthur* ensured its survival.

Other mediaeval tales of Troy, Alexander and the Romans were soon to be eclipsed by the revival of classical studies; and in England the Charlemagne cycle of stories which celebrated the triumph of Christendom over the infidel was to be superseded by the nationalist mood of the Elizabethans. The stories about King Arthur and his knights, on the other hand, were favoured and promoted by the Tudor monarchs to enhance the antiquity and renown of their house; but neither patriotism nor royal policy would have sufficed to keep alive the Arthurian romances if Malory had not retold them in a work of genius. To the difficult task of re-telling old tales Malory brought a blend of archaism and straightforwardness of style, of pathos and simplicity with ease and clarity.

Malory claims merely to be translating a French book, though in fact he used various sources, English and French, which he adapted to the requirements of his contemporaries. The Wars of the Roses made Englishmen look back nostalgically to the idealized chivalry of a remote past. Malory condensed his material; he eliminated the supernatural, as his main concern was with adventures and with conflicts of loyalty.

Caxton's edition of the *Morte d'Arthur* was completed on the last day of July 1485, three weeks before the defeat and death of Richard III at Bosworth Field. Caxton tells us that 'many noble and divers gentlemen' had often requested him to print the history of King Arthur. A copy of the Arthurian history was delivered to Caxton, 'which copy, Sir Thomas Malory did take out of certain books of French and reduced into English'. It contained all the elements of a best-seller in Caxton's day, or in any other: 'noble chivalry, courtesy, humanity . . . love, friendship, cowardice, murder, hate, virtue and sin'. The book is 'pleasant to read in, but for to give faith and believe that all is true that is contained herein, ye be at your liberty'.

To make his text more readable and clarify the narrative structure Caxton replaced difficult and

stronge þ þ myght but selde knyghtys stonde hym a buffette w
a spere   And at þ nexte feste sir Pelleas and sir charcarte
were made knyghtys of þ rounde table. ffor þ were .ij. segis
voyde for .ij. knyghtys were slayne þ yer. mony. And grete
Joy had kynge Arthure of sir Pelleas and off sir agauale
te But Pelleas loved never aftur sir Gawayne But as
he spared hym for þ love off þ kynge but oftyn tymes at
Justis & at turnementys sir Pelleas quytte sir Gawayne
for so hit recordyth in þe booke off ffrensh. So sir Trystrams many dayes aftur foughth w sir charcaute in an
Ilande and þ they dud a grete batayle But þ laste sir
Trystrams slew hym. So sir Trystrams was so woū
ded þ vnnethe he myght recou and lay at a Nunrye
halff a yere   And sir Pelleas was a worshyppfull
knyght and was one off þ iiij þt enchevyd þ Sankgreall.
And þ damesell off þ laake made by her meanes that nevir
he had a do w sir launcelot de laake ffor wher sir launce
lot was at ony Justis or at ony turnemente she wolde
nott suffer hym to be þ that day but yff hit were on þ syde
off sir launcelot. here endyth this tale as þ ffrensshe
booke seyth fro the marryage off kynge Uther vnto kynge
Arthure that regned aftur hym & dud many batayles
    And this booke endyth where as sir launcelot and
sir Trystrams com to courte. Who that woll make
ony more lette hym seke oþ bookes off kynge Arthure
or off sir launcelot or sir Trystrams ffor this was
drawyn by a knyght presoner sir Thomas Malleorre
that god sende hym good recou. Amen &c.

                    ¶Explicit

book of kynge Arthur & of his noble knyghtes of the rounde
table/that whan they were hole togyders there was euer an C
and xl/and here is the ende of the deth of Arthur /I praye
you all Ientyl men and Ientyl wymmen that redeth this book
of Arthur and his knyghtes from the begynnyng to the en
dynge / praye for me whyle I am on lyue that god sende me
good delyueraunce/& whan I am deed I praye you all praye
for my soule/for this book was ended the ix yere of the reygne
of kynge edward the fourth/by syr Thomas Maleoir knyght
as Ihesu helpe hym for hys grete myght/as he is the seruaunt
of Ihesu bothe day and nyght /

¶ Thus endeth thys noble and Ioyous book entytled le morte
Darthur/Notwythstondynge it treateth of the byrth/lyf/and
actes of the sayd kynge Arthur/of his noble knyghtes of the
rounde table/theyr meruayllous enquestes and aduentures /
thachyeuyng of the sangreal/ & in thende the dolorous deth &
departyng out of thys world of them al /whiche book was re
duced in to englysshe by syr Thomas Malory knyght as afore
is sayd /and by me deuyded in to xxi bookes chapytred and
enprynted /and fynysshed in thabbey westmestre the last day
of Iuyl the yere of our lord /M/CCCC/lxxxv /

¶ Caxton me fieri fecit

Caxton's colophon. Malory, Le Morte d'Arthur (Pierpont Morgan Library).

archaic words with words currently used; he re-wrote Book V, and divided the whole into shorter books and chapters with rubrics to summarize the action.

The copy exhibited is the only perfect copy; one other copy is known, that in the John Rylands University Library of Manchester.

73 *La mort darthur.*

Wynkyn de Worde: London, 1529. STC 803. G.10510.

The *Morte d'Arthur* was reprinted by Wynkyn de Worde in 1498 in a folio edition illustrated with woodcuts. (The unique surviving copy is in the John Rylands University Library of Manchester.) Wynkyn de Worde printed a second edition in 1529, using the 1498 woodcuts with some substitutions: the single copy surviving is shown here.

74 The Malory Manuscript.

Add. MS 59678.

This, the only known manuscript of the *Morte d'Arthur*, was discovered in the Fellows' Library at Winchester College in 1934 by Dr Walter Oakeshott. It was purchased from the College by the British Library earlier this year.

The manuscript, which is written on paper and probably dates from about 1484, is the work of two scribes, the first of whom was probably trained in law hand, though he is here writing a form of secretary. One gathering is missing at either end of the volume, and any early evidence of ownership which there may once have been has now disappeared. The book was rebound about 1800 and again as recently as 1948.

There are many variant readings between the text in this manuscript and the text printed by Caxton and it is often difficult to decide which reading is the more authoritative. In his edition of the *Works of Sir Thomas Malory* (Oxford, 1947; second edition 1967) Professor E. Vinaver concluded that the two both descended independently from Malory's original manuscript, by means of intermediate copies. Amongst the passages found in the manuscript but not in the printed text is one in which Sir Thomas Malory describes himself as a 'knyght presoner' (at the foot of the left-hand exhibited page, f.70b). His actual identity remains a mystery. A number of candidates have been put forward, but none can yet be regarded as absolutely convincing.

In 1975 Dr Lotte Hellinga detected printer's ink on the manuscript and, on f.186b, faint traces of three defective letters in mirrored type. Photographs taken under ultra-violet light confirmed that these are offsets from freshly-printed pages of letters which may possibly match Caxton's type 4*, in use from 1483 on, which is the type of his *Morte d'Arthur*. Furthermore a torn leaf of the manuscript (f.243) was once repaired with a piece of printer's waste, part of an Indulgence printed by Caxton in 1489 on vellum. These discoveries suggest that Caxton could have had the Malory Manuscript in his printing office and therefore that he might have used it in preparing the text which he eventually printed. It was not, however, used directly as printer's copy.

75 *Indulgence.*

[Printed 1489.] Type 7. Duff 212. STC 14101. From Add. MS 59678.

This fragment of an Indulgence, printed on vellum, was discovered in the Malory Manuscript, pasted to the lower part of f.243b in order to effect a repair to a long tear in the page. It was raised in 1934, since when it has been preserved separately.

The Indulgence was issued by Johannes de Gigliis and Perseus de Malviciis in the name of Pope Innocent VIII. Only one complete copy of this setting is known; this is in the library of Trinity College, Dublin. The other setting is also exhibited (83).

Caxton and the Tudors

Soon after his victory at Bosworth on 22 August 1485 Henry VII married the Princess Elizabeth, daughter of Edward IV and Queen Elizabeth Woodville, on 18 January 1486. It was not until three years later that Caxton was offered or accepted Tudor patronage. His choice of texts in the meanwhile shows that, in an endeavour to find new customers, he abandoned the English poets and his own translations and turned to standard school books and devotional works, books he could sell without patronage.

76 *The Life of Charles the Great*. Translated by Caxton.
Printed 1 December 1485.
Type 4*. Duff 83. STC 5013.
C.10.b.9. (De Ricci 19:1).

The anonymous French original of Caxton's translation was actually a recent compilation by John Bagnyon of Lausanne and Geneva, consisting mainly of his prose adaptation of *Fierabras*, a verse romance of the Charlemagne cycle telling how the Saracen giant Fierabras was defeated by Olivier and converted to Christianity. This completed Caxton's publication of the histories of the three Christian Worthies. The British Library copy is the only one known,

Caxton states that *Charles the Great* was commissioned by 'some persons of noble estate and degree', in particular 'a good and singular friend of mine Master William Daubeny, one of the Treasurers of the Jewels of . . . our sovereign lord late of noble memory King Edward IV'.

Daubeny in 1480 also obtained the lucrative sinecure of Searcher in the Port of London, which he retained under Richard III. He had just lost both posts under Henry VII and Caxton may have been trying to put in a good word for him.

77 *The history of the noble and valiant knight Paris and the fair Vienne*. Translated by Caxton.
Printed 19 December 1485.
Type 4*. Duff 337. STC 19206.
C.10.b.10. (De Ricci 83:1)

This is the only known copy of Caxton's translation (from an abridgment of a French text written in 1432) of a putative Provençal tale about the troubadour knight Paris and the princess Vienne.

An edition in French was published soon afterwards by Gerard Leeu at Antwerp in 1487, from a manuscript closely related to Caxton's. Leeu had printed the Dutch *Reynard the Fox* in 1479 two years before Caxton's English edition, for which Leeu may have supplied the copy. Just after Caxton's death Leeu reprinted three of Caxton's publications in the English language (*Jason*, *Paris and Vienne*, and *Chronicles of England*), probably by arrangement with Caxton's executors or his successor, Wynkyn de Worde.

78 Clement Maydestone: *Directorium sacerdotum*. First edition.
[Printed 1486.] Type 5. Duff 290. STC 17720.
C.10.b.16. (De Ricci 77:1)

This is the only known complete copy.

The *Directorium* is a revised version of the Sarum *Ordinal* which Caxton had produced for sale 'good cheap' at the Red Pale seven years earlier. It was compiled about 1450 by Clement Maydestone, a member of the Brigittine community at Syon in Middlesex, who died in 1456. By the end of the fifteenth century his version was regarded as standard.

At the beginning of the book is inserted the single sheet folio woodcut 'The Image of Pity' (De Ricci 54; STC 14072). 'Image of Pity' cuts evolved from manuscript miniatures of the Mass of St Gregory, which depict the Saint saying mass and seeing a vision of the dead Christ with the instruments of the Passion.

This cut has a manuscript label over the excised original printed text (an offer of indulgence). The *Directorium* is not, as the label says, Caxton's only Latin text.

79 *The Royal Book*. Translation by Caxton completed 13 September 1484.
[Printed 1486–7.] Type 5. Duff 366. STC 21429.
C.10.b.22. (De Ricci 89:7)

This is the only Book printed in Latin by Caxton, and which is not mention'd in any Catalogue of his Works. It confutes a Notion that has commonly obtained, that he confined himself to the printing of English.

Dr Middleton's Dissertation on the Origin of Printing

(78) The 'Image of Pity'.

Caxton's *Royal Book* is a translation of *La Somme le Roy*, treatises on the Vices and Virtues compiled in 1279 by the Dominican Frère Laurent for Philip III, *le Hardi*, King of France, to whom he was confessor. The translation was made at the request of an unnamed Mercer friend. This work, which includes passages on the Creed and the Ten Commandments, enjoyed considerable popularity during the late Middle Ages. An English version, the *Ayenbite of Inwyt*, was produced as early as 1340. The original French version came to be embellished with a series of illustrations and two magnificently illuminated copies (Add. MSS 28162 and 54180) may be seen in the permanent exhibition in the Grenville Library.

80 *The Life of the holy and blessed virgin Saint Winifred*. Translated by Caxton from the Latin text of Robert of Shrewsbury, written about 1140.

[Printed 1485? or 1487?.]
Type 4*. Duff 414. STC 25853.
C.10.b.89. (De Ricci 100:2)

The Welsh Saint Winifred was beheaded in 636 A.D. by Prince Cradock, while defending her virtue. The prince fell suddenly dead and was carried away by fiends; Winifred's head, however, was miraculously restored, with 'only a little redness in manner of a thread' to mark the join.

Caxton's book, which included the text of the services for her feast day as celebrated at Shrewsbury Abbey, was probably commissioned by the Abbey for sale to pilgrims.

Caxton's imports of books

Before printing began in England, it is known that some printed books were imported into this country. The London Customs Accounts preserved in the Public Record Office, however, only mention this trade in books for the first time on 30 December 1477.

For general merchandise, which included books, 3d in the £ was levied upon the value of alien exports and imports. In addition both English and foreign merchants had to pay a subsidy on exports and imports of all merchandise, unless they were merchants of the Hanseatic towns: Hamburg, Lübeck, Danzig, Bremen and Cologne.

On 25 February 1488 Caxton brought to London 112 books to the value of £13 on board the *Garden Avyse*, which carried merchandise for one other English merchant and for a Spaniard. On 25 April 1488 he imported books which had a total value of £10 16s 8d on board a ship of which Richard Harvy was ship-master, which also carried timber. The same day Caxton brought to London with the shipmaster Thomas Payn 1049 volumes to a value of £17 5s. In the same year Caxton also exported books from London. On 10 December the following entry appears in the London Customs Accounts: 'In the ship of John Garny, of William Caxton, denizen, for 1 box with 140 volumes printed in French, value £6'.

It is possible that these books were remainder copies of *Recueil des histoires de Troie*, *Les Faits de Jason*, *Les méditations sur les sept Psaumes* and *Les quatre dernières choses*, all printed by Caxton in French in Bruges. Caxton may also have tried to sell in England books printed by others on the continent, e.g. by Guillaume Maynyal.

We cannot tell whether Caxton carried on this trade before 1488 or whether he continued it after this date. Unfortunately the Customs Accounts never mention where a ship came from or its destination.

Caxton's device

Usually printed after the colophon, devices or printers' marks have been used from the very beginning of printing. As printer and publisher were often the same man, this soon turned them also into publishers' devices, the purpose of which was to serve as a hall-mark of quality and to safeguard what later became known as copyright. Such marks were in common use in

(**88**) *Caxton's device*. Book of
Eneydos, *1490*.

Caxton's time and later, not by printers alone,
for marking bales of merchandise and similar
purposes; the marks scratched by masons on
their buildings had the same purpose.

The design of Caxton's device is bold and
effective. The printer's initials are on either side
of a device incorporating the numbers '4' and '7'.
The lines are so drawn and orientated as to read
either '47' or '74': the year 1447 would presumably refer to his obtaining freedom of the
Mercers' Company; and 1474 the year in which
he issued his first book, according to Flanders
dating. The decoration of the borders, with the
interlocking foliage, flowers, and white on black

is in the style of the Gouda woodcutter who supplied Caxton, Gerard Leeu and other printers
with woodcut initials.

On its appearance in the *Sarum Missal*,
4 December 1487, the bottom frameline of
Caxton's device already showed a 10 mm gap at
the right-hand end. In the *Sarum Legenda*, 14
August 1488, there was another gap in the device
6 mm to the left of the first. During 1489 further
damage occurred, and so on to 1491. G. D.
Painter has used the six stages of deterioration,
taken with other evidence, to assign inferential
dates to the ten undated books in which the
device appears.

81 *Missale ad usum Sarum.*

Printed for William Caxton by Guillaume Maynyal: Paris, 4 December 1487.

Duff 322, De Ricci 102. STC 16164.

Lent anonymously.

Caxton printed a number of service-books of the Sarum Use on his own press at Westminster, such as the *Hours* and Maydestone's *Directorium*. Why did he go to the trouble and expense of having the *Missal* and the *Legenda* printed abroad by Maynyal? The reasons almost certainly lie in his inability to execute adequately the large amount of red printing necessary for the rubrics in these books.

At Bruges Caxton's red printing was done at one pull instead of two: all the type was inked in black; the 'red' type was then wiped clean and re-inked in red – the re-inking was apparently done by means of ink-balls, as black print an inch or more away from the red has been reddened. The result was marred also by the dismal appearance of the red print, thus contaminated by a black undercoat. In the last few years of his life at Westminster Caxton's red printing, which appears in three books only, was competently done by the normal two-pull process though on a smaller scale than in the books he had earlier entrusted to Maynyal. Maynyal's other known productions are noted for their fine red printing, and this is why Caxton had his *Missal* printed abroad by him. Caxton's successor Wynkyn de Worde was no more able to produce such a missal on his own; his *Sarum Missal* of 1496 was printed for him in London by Julian Notary and Jean Barbier.

This is in fact the first missal printed in Paris with the rubrics printed in red. The staves only of the music are printed; the portion of the marriage service in English is written in by hand.

A copy was presented by Caxton himself to the shrine of Edward the Confessor at Westminster Abbey; the gift is recorded in an inventory of 1520. This copy no longer survives, and the copy exhibited, which contains 243 out of a total of 266 leaves, is the only one known, apart from fragments.

Caxton's imports in the spring of 1488 may have included the *Sarum Missal* printed by Maynyal, though the value of these books seems too low; unless Caxton for customs purposes undervalued his books. The *Missal* contains Caxton's name in the colophon as well as his device, which appears here for the first time. William Blades suggested that the device was specially made for the *Missal* because Caxton's name in the colophon might easily be overlooked. The block was probably cut abroad and the impressions executed at Westminster after the importation of the books from Paris. It was used by Caxton in ten other books between 1489 and 1491 and by Wynkyn de Worde after him until 1531.

82 *Legenda ad usum Sarum*

Printed for Caxton by Guillaume Maynyal: Paris, 14 August 1488. Duff 247, De Ricci 101. STC 16136.

IB 40010

The *Legenda*, or lectionary, is a service-book containing the lessons of the Breviary, i.e. the readings from the Bible, the lives of the Saints and homilies, appropriate to each day of the Church's year.

This copy comprises 351 leaves; the original total probably exceeded 372. The loss of leaves seems fortuitous rather than due to the removal, in the sixteenth century, of passages repugnant to the reformed Church. On the other hand, in accordance with Archbishop Cranmer's amendment forced through Convocation in 1542, the word 'Papa' has been struck out with a pen throughout the book, and whole passages relating to St Thomas à Becket have been obliterated.

The inner forme of sheet C presents two features of interest: first, C2 verso has been used for proof and is marked up accordingly; secondly, on its opposite page in the forme, C7 recto, the black printing proper to this page has been superimposed over red printing proper to C2 verso, but printed with differences in spacing and punctuation from the setting to be found there. C7 recto, if correctly printed, would be solid

(83) Indulgence, *1489*.

black, as the text here requires no rubrics and therefore no printing in red.

The text appropriate to C2 verso, both black and red, was by mistake set up twice over. The red text of the forme was then printed first, as was usual. When the error, i.e. that both pages contained the same rubrics, was noticed, C7 recto was then correctly re-set in its solid black text, and the black printing completed. Instead of being discarded for waste, however, this sheet was used for proof. Lastly, either by another error or for the sake of economy, the same sheet was used to make up this copy of the book. Elsewhere, apart from a few examples of faulty register, the black and red printing of the *Legenda* is good.

Survivals of fifteenth-century proof are rare, and usually occur as printers' waste found in bindings. If this proof-page, which calls for some twenty corrections, is typical, there would have been about 15,000 corrections in the whole work; Caxton's contract with the French printer Maynyal may have included severe penalties for misprints. The d-sign for deletion is not used by Maynyal's corrector, who uses a v-sign as in line 17. A caret-sign occurs at the end of line 29 where a question-mark is to be inserted. There are extensive marginalia elsewhere in a contemporary hand, sometimes giving the sources of the printed lessons, e.g. near the foot of the left-hand margin of C2 verso.

The *Legenda* is the only one of Caxton's productions of which the published price, or at least the market value about ten years later, are known. In 1496 as part of the separation settlement between Caxton's daughter Elizabeth and her husband Gerard Crop, a merchant tailor, the latter was awarded twenty 'prynted legendes' valued at 13*s* 4*d* each, a poor substitute for the £80 'in ready money', which Crop asserted that Caxton, 'lying in his death bed', had bequeathed to him. In 1496 also the Churchwardens of St Margaret's Westminster owned fifteen copies of 'bokes called a legende' at the bequest of William Caxton. These they sold at five or six shillings apiece and by 1502 or so they had only one copy left.

This unique copy, purchased by the British Museum in 1957, was discovered by Paul Morgan in the Library of St Mary's, Warwick in 1956. Caxton's *Legenda* was previously known only from twenty-nine leaves in the University Library, Cambridge and from ten odd leaves elsewhere.

(84) Faytes of arms, *1489*. (Opposite.)

Here begynneth the book of fayttes of armes ⁊ of Chyual-
rpe/And the first chapytre is the prologue/in whiche ypry-
styne of pyse excuseth hir self to haue dar enterpryse to speke
of so hye matere as is conteyned in this sayd book

⁋ Capitulum primum

By cause that hardynes is so moche necessarye to
entrepryse hye thynges/whiche without that
shold neu be enpryses That same is couenable
to me at this present werke to put it forth without other thyng/Seen the lytylhed of my per-
sone/whiche I knowe not digne ne worthy to treate of so
hye matere/ne durst not only thynke what blame hardynes
causeth whan she is folyssh/I thene nothyng moeued by ar-
rogauce in folyssh presupcion/but admonested of veray af-
feccion ⁊ good desyre of noble men in thoffyce of armes/am
exorted after myne other escriptures passed/lyke as he that
hath to forn beten doun many stronge edyfices/is more hardy
to charge hym self defpe or to bete doun a castell or forteresse
whan he feleth hym self garnysshed of couenable stuffe therto
necessarye/Thenne to entrepryse to speke in this present book
of the right honorable offyce of armes ⁊ of Chyualrye/as
wel in thynges whiche therto ben conuenyent/as in droytes
whyche therto be appertenaunt/lyke as the lawes ⁊ dyuerse
auctours declaren it/to the purpoos/I haue assembled the maters ⁊ gadred in dyuerse bokes for to produce myne entencio
in this present volume/But as it apperteyneth this matere
to be more executed by fayt of dyligece ⁊ witte/than by sub-
tyltees of wordes polisshed/and also considered that they that
ben excersyng ⁊ experte in tharte of chyualrye be not comune-
ly clerkys ne instructe in science of langage/I entende not
to treate/but to the most playn and entendible langage that

A i

Caxton's new patrons

The *Fours Sons of Aymon* [1488], was translated from the French by Caxton to the commission of his new patron John de Vere, Earl of Oxford, 'my singular and especial lord' who was then the most powerful magnate in England. Caxton dedicated to Lady Margaret Beaufort, mother of Henry VII, his edition of the thirteenth-century romance *Blanchardin and Eglantine*. Unique copies of both these books are in the John Rylands University Library of Manchester.

At Winchester on 19 September 1486 Henry VII's Queen Elizabeth bore him a son and heir, Prince Arthur, for whom the Earl of Oxford stood godfather and Queen Elizabeth Woodville godmother. Caxton's *Eneydos* is dedicated to the young Prince Arthur, in the same terms as he had dedicated the *History of Jason* to the unfortunate Prince Edward. Caxton had with *Faytes of Arms* already reached Henry himself.

83 *Indulgence*. (A single half leaf.)
[Printed not after 24 April 1489.]
Type 7. Duff 211. STC 14100.
IA 55126 (De Ricci 60:1)

Issued 24 April 1489 to Henry Bost, Provost of Eton, and sometime confessor to Edward IV's favourite mistress Jane Shore; her divorced husband was Caxton's fellow Mercer, William Shore.

84 Christine de Pisan: *The Faytes of Arms and of Chivalry*. Translation by Caxton.
Printed 14 July 1489.
Type 6. Duff 96. STC 7269.
G. 10546. (De Ricci 28:4); another copy:
IB 55131 (De Ricci 28:10)

Under his new patron the Earl of Oxford, Caxton obtained his first commission from Henry VII: this was *Faytes of Arms* by Christine de Pisan (who also wrote *Moral Proverbs*, printed by Caxton for Earl Rivers in 1478).

Faytes of Arms, a treatise on the art and rules of war, although compiled in 1408–9 and based on the classical military writer, Vegetius, was brought up to date with information on gunnery, siegecraft, etc., and therefore of some practical use. Christine herself admitted that her subject was a 'thing not accustomed to women which commonly . . . spin on the distaff and occupy them in things of household'.

The manuscript of the French original, delivered to Caxton by the king through the Earl was not, as has been suggested, Royal MS 15 E. vi. This manuscript, given in 1445 to Margaret of Anjou, apparently as a wedding present, by John Talbot, Earl of Shrewsbury, understandably omits Christine's allegation that the Black Prince, in 1367, murdered the French envoys, which, surprisingly enough, is present in Caxton's version.

Caxton, as he was expected to do, made topical references to Henry's 'noble and most redoubted enterprises as well in Brittany, Flanders and other places . . . I have not heard nor read that any prince has subdued his subjects with less hurt'.

85 Christine de Pisan: *Le livre des fays d'armes*.
Harley MS 4605.

This manuscript copy of the original French text of Christine de Pisan's treatise on the art and rules of war was written and illuminated in London in 1434. The scribe who wrote it seems to have been a Frenchman, though working in an English tradition, and the decoration of the book is strongly influenced by contemporary French illumination. This copy does include the passage detrimental to the reputation of the Black Prince, omitted from Royal MS 15 E. vi.

The exhibited miniature shows a prince ordering a merchant into prison (ff.94b–95), and introduces the last book of the work.

86 *The Doctrinal of Sapience*. Translated by Caxton.
[Printed after 7 May 1489.]
Type 5. Duff 127. STC 21431.
IB 55129 (De Ricci 40:6)

fayn wolde I satysfye euery man/ and so to do toke an olde
boke and redde therin/ and certaynly the englysshe was so ru
de and brood that I coude not wele vnderstande it. And also
my lorde abbot of westmynster ded do shewe to me late certa:
yn euydences wryton in olde englysshe for to reduce it in to
our englysshe now vsid/ And certaynly it was wreton in
suche wyse that it was more lyke to dutche than englysshe
I coude not reduce ne brynge it to be vnderstonden/ And cer:
taynly our langage now vsed varyeth ferre from that. Whi
che was vsed and spoken whan I was borne/ For we en:
glysshe men/ ben borne vnder the domynacyon of the mone.
Whiche is neuer stedfaste/ but euer wauerynge/ wexynge o:
ne season/ and waneth & dyscreaseth another season/ And
that comyn englysshe that is spoken in one shyre varyeth
from a nother. In so moche that in my dayes happened that
certayn marchauntes were in a ship in tamyse for to haue
sayled ouer the see into zelande/ and for lacke of wynde thei
taryed atte forlond. and wente to lande for to refresshe them
And one of theym named sheffelde a mercer cam in to an
hows and axed for mete. and specyally he axyd after eggys
And the good wyf answerde. that she coude speke no fren:
she. And the marchaut was angry. for he also coude speke
no frensshe. but wolde haue hadde egges/ and she vnderstode
hym not/ And thenne at laste a nother sayd that he wolde
haue eyren/ then the good wyf sayd that she vnderstod hym
wel/ Loo what sholde a man in thyse dayes now wryte. eg:
ges or eyren/ certaynly it is harde to playse euery man/ by
cause of dyuersite & chaunge of langage . For in these dayes
euery man that is in ony reputacyon in his countre. wyll vt
ter his comynycacyon and maters in suche maners & ter:
mes/ that fewe men shall vnderstonde theym/ And som ho:

(88) *The story of the good wife and the eggs. Prologue*, The Book of Eneydos, *1490.*

Caxton's translation of a manual of popular theology, with anecdotes, is similar to the *Royal Book*, from which in fact the anonymous French author lifted parts of his material. In the *Doctrinal of Sapience*, however, Caxton did not repeat his earlier version of these parts, but translated them afresh.

87 *Statutes 1, 3, 4 of King Henry VII.*
[Printed 1490.] Type 6. Duff 380. STC 9348.
G. 6002. (De Ricci 93:2)

Having renewed his connection with the Crown, Caxton was entrusted with printing the statutes of Henry's first three Parliaments. The Statutes of England had hitherto always appeared in Law French, and now William de Machlinia who had printed Richard's *Statutes* (in French) was no longer in business. G. D. Painter suggests that as Caxton was then the only printer in England and he held no stock of type with the special contractions required for Law French, Henry's *Statutes* had to be printed in English.

After Caxton's death Wynkyn de Worde retained his monopoly of the Statutes, which continued to appear in English; while Pynson produced the law reports or *Year Books*, for which Law French remained obligatory.

88 *The Book of Eneydos.* Translation by Caxton of the *Livre des Énéides.*
[Printed after 22 June 1490.]
Type 6. Duff 404. STC 24796.
C.10.b.12. (De Ricci 96:6); another copy:
G. 9723. (De Ricci 96:8)

This is a translation, not of Virgil's *Aeneid*, but (as Caxton tells us in his prologue) of 'a little book in French', a late fourteenth century romance adapted from Virgil and from Boccaccio's *De casibus virorum illustrium*. The Scottish poet Gavin Douglas condemned this paraphrase and by way of a corrective to it undertook his own translation of the Latin original.

Eneydos is dedicated to Prince Arthur. Caxton was no humanist, and he knew it: he appealed to the leading poet 'Master John Skelton . . . to

oversee and correct this said book . . . For he hath late translated . . . not in rude and old language but in polished and ornate terms craftily, as he that hath read Virgil, Ovid, Tully and all the other noble poets and orators to me unknown'.

Caxton's English style

Caxton had been constantly apologizing ever since the *Recuyell* for his 'rude and common English' – 'there be no gay terms nor subtle nor new eloquence', he said of *Charles the Great* – but by these 'humility formulas' he really meant the opposite. Indeed, his translations of chivalric romances especially were adorned to excess with 'such gay terms as now be said in these days'. In his prologue to the *Eneydos*, one of the last pieces he wrote, Caxton freely admits this: he tells us of the pleasure he took in the style of the French original, and how he 'concluded to translate it into English and forthwith . . . wrote a leaf or twain, which I oversaw again to correct it. And when I saw the fair and strange terms therein I doubted that it should not please some gentlemen which late blamed me, saying that in my translation I had over curious terms which could not be understood of common people and desired me to use old and homely terms.' 'Fain would I satisfy every man', Caxton goes on, 'and so to do took an old book and read therein, and certainly the English was so rude and broad that I could not well understand it.' He gives further examples. 'And some honest and great clerks have . . . desired me to write the most curious terms that I could find, and thus between plain rude and curious I stand abashed . . . therefore in a mean between both I have reduced and translated this said book into our English.'

89 *Speculum vitae Christi.* ('The Mirror of the Life of Christ', formerly attributed to St Bonaventura.) Second edition.
[Printed 1490.] Type 5. Duff 49. STC 3260.
IB 55119 (De Ricci 10:1)

Corpus Christi

Pentecost.

(**89**) *Woodcuts from* Speculum vitae Christi, *1490.*

This immensely popular life of Christ, former-ly attributed to St Bonaventura (1221–74), is now considered to be the work of another Franciscan, Johannes de Caulibus of San Gimi-gnano. It was translated into English about 1410 by Nicholas Love, the Carthusian prior of Mount Grace of Ingleby in Yorkshire; it remained current for over a century, and was recommend-ed by Sir Thomas More in his *Apology*.

This is Caxton's second edition, a close reprint in the same type of his first edition of 1486, of which the only surviving copy is in the Cam-bridge University Library.

The woodcuts which illustrate both editions are superior to the relatively coarse work pro-duced by the two artists previously employed by Caxton. He probably ordered them from Flanders in 1485; the twenty-five cuts of the Life of Christ are French in style.

This copy, printed on vellum, was before the Reformation in the Brigittine nunnery at Syon. It is one of the only three known copies of any Caxton edition printed on vellum apart from indulgences and a *Donatus* fragment.

90 *The Art and craft to know well to die.* **Translated by** Caxton from an abridgement of the *Ars moriendi*.
[Printed after 15 June 1490.]
Type 6. Duff 35. STC 789.
C.11.c.8. (De Ricci 6:1)

If the Maude Caxton whose burial in 1490 is recorded in the Churchwardens' accounts of St Margaret's, Westminster was in fact Caxton's wife, it may have been in connection with this event that Caxton interrupted his translation of *Eneydos* to translate the *Art of Dying*. It is a com-pilation of meditations, exhortations and prayers for the dying and those attending them. Caxton's translation, finished on 15 June 1490, was made from a French abridgement of one of the many Latin recensions of a text then in great demand.

91 *Governal of health* and *Medicina stomachi*.
[Printed 1491.] Type 6. Duff 165. STC 12138.
(De Ricci 47:6)
Lent by the Curators of the Bodleian Library.

Soon after his book on the art of dying Caxton produced one on how to keep alive, an anonymous fifteenth-century translation of the *Regimen sanitatis*. This popular compilation of simple rules for health was not the earliest medical book to be printed in English – this was the *Treatise on the Pestilence*, printed by William de Machlinia about 1486. *The Governal of Health* is followed by 'Medicine for the stomach', in English verse now accepted as the work of John Lydgate. His closing observation is:

To feeble stomach when they cannot refrain
From thing contrary to their complexion
Of greedy hands the stomach hath great pain . . .
Moderate food giveth to man his health.

Lydgate concludes:

This receipt bought is of no apothecary
Of Master Anthony nor of Master Hugh
To all indifferent it is richest dietary
Explicit medicina stomachi.

92 *Book of divers ghostly matters:* Horologium sapientiae; the XII Profits of tribulation; The Rule of Saint Benedict.
[Printed 1491.] Type 6. Duff 55. STC 3305.
IA 55141. (De Ricci 12:2)

Caxton evidently printed the collective volume as it reached him, 'by desiring of certain worshipful persons', probably of the Benedictine Order.

'The whole content of this little book is not of one matter only', but is made up of three sections: *The Seven Points of True Love*, an English version of the *Horologium sapientiae*, written about 1340 by the Dominican mystic Henry Suso; the anonymous *Twelve profits of tribulation*; and the Rule of St Benedict in English. Each section has separate signatures, and each finishes, as if it were complete, with a colophon or with Caxton's device. The three sections are therefore capable of standing alone; this probably encouraged the

thief who stole the *Twelve profits* from the copy which had earlier belonged to the English Benedictine nuns of Our Lady of Good Hope in Paris. It was reunited in 1938 with the first part of the book, which had been acquired by the British Museum in 1898.

93 *Ars moriendi.* Translation from the Latin, possibly by Caxton.
[Printed 1491.] Types 6 and 8. Duff 33. STC 786.
(De Ricci 5:1)
Lent by the Curators of the Bodleian Library.

The only known copy of Caxton's edition of a shorter version of the *Art to know well to die*, the death-bed tract which was often printed in various languages and countries in the fifteenth century:

When any of likelihood shall die, then it is most necessary to have a special friend the which will heartily help and pray for him.

94 *The Fifteen Oes and other prayers.*
[Printed 1491.]
Type 6. Duff 150. STC 20195.
IA 55144 (De Ricci 44:1); another copy;
IB 55144A (De Ricci 44:2)

This collection of prayers was printed by Caxton at the command of Henry VII's consort Queen Elizabeth and of his mother, Lady Margaret Beaufort. The text is mostly in Latin but begins with an English translation of the Fifteen Oes, prayers wrongly attributed to St Bridget of Sweden (c.1303–73), each of which begins with the vocative 'O'.

The first copy is the only complete one. The second copy is a fragment of four leaves, discarded and used as the lower pastedown by Caxton's binder in the Bristol Baptist College copy of the *Mirror of the World* (now 102, IB 55142). It consists of the inner half-sheet of quire a (a3–6), and is an example of wrong imposition, a not infrequent mishap in Caxton's office.

The inner forme (a3–a6) was imposed upside down, thus giving the wrong page sequence. When the error was noticed the type of the outer forme had already been distributed and so it was

(**94**) The Fifteen Oes, *1491.*

necessary to reprint this half-sheet in correct imposition, using a new setting of the outer forme
and the still standing type of the inner forme.
Hence the outer forme is an entirely different
setting with a different choice of border pieces
from the corresponding forme in the only complete copy (IB 55144).

Each forme of the fragment bears a different
offset impression from two otherwise unknown
editions by Caxton of the Sarum *Horae*, one
quarto, the other octavo.

95 *Vitas patrum.* (In English.)

Westminster: Wynkyn de Worde, before
21 August 1495. Duff 235. STC 14507.

C.11.b.3.

Caxton at the age of nearly seventy was at work
on his second longest translation, *Vitas patrum*, a
collection of lives of the Desert Fathers, wrongly

ascribed to Saint Jerome, 'late translated out of
Latin into French and diligently corrected [and
printed] in the city of Lyons'.

He did not live to see his last translation in
print. Wynkyn de Worde published it in 1495,
remarking 'it was in the year of Our Lord 1491
reduced into English' and that Caxton 'finished
it at the last day of his life'.

(**90**) *Colophon.* The art and craft to know well to die,
1490.

[87]

(**96**) *Death and the printers. In* La grante danse macabre. *Lyons, 1499.*

96 'Death and the Printers.'

In *La grante danse macabre*, Lyons, 1499.

IB 41735.

The earliest known representation of a printing shop. On the left of the picture we see Death leading off a compositor and two pressmen. On the right in a cubicle built into the main room we see a man behind the counter; there are books (all bound) on the counter and on the shelves behind him. Caxton's shop may have been like this.

The compositor (left) holds in his left hand a composing stick in which he is arranging types taken from the compartments on the trestle table. The text he is setting is supported by a stick fixed to the table.

On the bench beside him is a two-page forme which he is setting up. The forme would be inked (by the man with the ink-balls in his hands), placed on the platen of the press, and printed when the pulling of the handle (by the man in front of the press) pressed the inked formes on to the paper.

Caxton's death

The biennial Churchwardens' accounts of St Margaret's Westminster for May 1490 to May 1492 contain an entry for Caxton's funeral, which cost more than twice as much as Maude Caxton's in 1490. (A photograph is shown here.)

Caxton's will does not survive, but we know that he left copies of the *Sarum Legenda* to St Margaret's, probably to pay for 'obits' or prayers for his soul. He left his business and equipment to Wynkyn de Worde, who after about six months resumed printing, using Caxton's types, initials and woodcuts, and his device.

Towards the beginning of 1492 Richard Pynson began to print in London; one of his first books in that year was an edition of the *Canterbury Tales* in which he referred to 'my worshipful master William Caxton'. Pynson was very likely trained and worked under Caxton, and set up his own business after Caxton's death. The demand which Caxton had promoted for English books grew; Wynkyn de Worde and Pynson prospered for over four decades.

Wynkyn de Worde

Wynkyn de Worde, a native of Wörth in Alsace, was certainly in Caxton's employ soon after the press was set up at Westminster, and may have worked for him in Bruges. Some of his best books owe everything to Caxton: his editions of the English translation of the *Golden Legend* (1493, 97) and two further editions of the *Canterbury Tales*. About two-fifths of Wynkyn's great output was intended for the use of schools; he was the first English publisher to make printed school books the financial basis of his business.

Wynkyn de Worde, the most prolific of all the early English printers, had none of his master Caxton's gifts as translator or editor; he was simply a businessman, concerning himself entirely with printing and book-selling. By 1535, the year of his death, he had brought out about 600 books. For his first two years as independent printer Wynkyn used Caxton's old types, and introduced a new one of his own only in 1493, in the *Liber Festivalis* (Duff 307).

Richard Pynson

In 1500 Wynkyn moved to Fleet Street in London where other printers were already at work. One of them, Richard Pynson, a Norman by birth, had started printing in London in 1492 and remained in business until his death in 1530. During these years Pynson published some 400 books, technically and typographically the finest specimens of English printing of their period. They include the *Canterbury Tales* and much popular work in English, but Pynson's main publishing interest lay in the field of law-books.

97 Bartholomaeus Anglicus: *De proprietatibus rerum.* (In English.)
[Westminster]: Wynkyn de Worde, [1495.]
Duff 40. STC 1536.
G. 10565.

In the colophon to his English translation of Bartholomaeus Wynkyn de Worde notes that his master Caxton was 'first printer of this book, in Latin tongue at Cologne'. He goes on to point out that the book is printed on paper made in England; it is in fact the first book printed on English paper, made by John Tate the Younger.

The Bartholomaeus is typical of Wynkyn de Worde's best press-work. From 1500 on until his death in 1535 he increasingly aimed to supply a wider market with cheaper books in smaller format.

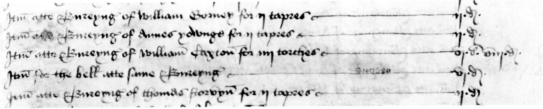

Record of Caxton's burial. St Margaret's, Westminster: Churchwardens' Accounts, 27 May 1490–3 June 1492. (Westminster City Libraries.)
Item atte Bureyng of William Caxton for iiii torches vi.s. viij.d.
Item for the bell atte same Bureyn ;   vi.d.

Bookbinding by the 'Caxton binder' and his contemporaries

The 'Caxton bindery' was at work in Westminster until c.1510. Of the thirty-six bindings known to have come from this shop, twenty-eight cover printed books, of which thirteen were printed by William Caxton and four by Wynkyn de Worde. In several of the bindings, leaves printed by Caxton or by Wynkyn de Worde have been found, which were originally used either to form or strengthen the boards, or as paste-downs. The fact that no waste from any other printer has been found in any of these bindings suggests that the binder may have been employed first by Caxton and after his death by Wynkyn de Worde; or at least, that he lived at Westminster and could easily have been supplied with printer's waste by Caxton and his successor.

Though this bindery was used by Caxton and may even have been under his control, it had by no means the monopoly of binding all Caxton's publications. Books printed by Caxton survive which were bound by other binders, such as the Dragon binder, W.G. and the Unicorn binder.

Examples of these last two binders' work are shown in the exhibition alongside twelve examples from the 'Caxton bindery' and a few bindings from other contemporary shops.

98 A binding by the 'Caxton binder'.
Chartulary of the Abbey of St Peter's Westminster. Fifteenth-century manuscript on vellum. fol.
Lent by the College of Arms, London.
C.G.Y.72.

Brown calf over wooden boards, tooled in blind to a panel design. The border of the panel is filled with round fleur-de-lis tools. The panel is divided by fillets into lozenges containing the arms of Thomas Beaufort, Earl of Dorset and 1st Duke of Exeter (d.1427), and half lozenges containing round fleur-de-lis tools. The outer border contains the same fleur-de-lis and arms tools and lozenge-shaped nosegay tools. Re-backed; traces of two pairs of clasps.

99 A binding by the 'Caxton binder'.
Chronica de regibus Anglie. Fifteenth-century manuscript on vellum. 8°.
Add. MS 10106.

Brown calf over wooden boards, tooled in blind to a panel design with fillets forming the panel. The border contains carrot tools and small rosettes and the panel is divided by a vertical strip, filled with rosettes into two halves, each filled with a row of carrot tools. Re-backed; traces of one pair of clasps.

100 A binding by the 'Caxton binder'.
Hymni ecclesiastici. Fifteenth-century manuscript on vellum. Small fol.
Lent by Chetham's Library, Manchester.
Mun. A3 129.

Brown leather over wooden boards, tooled in blind to a panel design. The border of the panel is filled with interlaced crescent tools and the panel is divided by fillets into lozenges containing square floral tools, and half lozenges containing fleur-de-lis tools. Re-backed; remnants of two pairs of clasps.

101 A binding by the Unicorn binder, c.1490.
Jacques Legrand: *The Book of good manners.* Translated by Caxton, 8 June 1486.
Westminster: W. Caxton, 11 May 1487. fol.
IB 55125. (De Ricci 65:4)

Brown calf over wooden boards, tooled in blind to a panel design. The border of the panel is filled with branch tools and square tools depicting a dromedary. The panel is divided by fillets into lozenges, containing triangular flower tools. Re-backed with the original back-strip onlaid; remnants of two pairs of clasps.

The Unicorn binder, so named after his most characteristic tool, worked between 1485 and 1504 and has been tentatively identified as

(**109**) *A binding by the 'Caxton binder'. Eusebius:* Historia ecclesiastica, *1506 (British Library: Henry Davis Gift)*.

Walter Hatley, a Cambridge binder (*fl.c.*1484–1504).

Jacques Legrand, an Augustinian friar in Paris wrote this treatise, *Le Livre des bonnes moeurs*, on the qualities desirable in princes and lords, secular and spiritual. Caxton's translation was done at the request of his Mercer friend, recently deceased, William Pratt, with whom he had taken livery in 1452.

102 A binding by the 'Caxton binder', *c.*1490.
The Mirror of the World. Second edition.
Westminster: W. Caxton, [1489]. fol.
IB 55142. (De Ricci 95:7)

Brown calf over wooden boards, tooled in blind to a panel design. The panel is divided by fillets into lozenges, which contain on the upper cover lozenge-shaped nosegay tools and on the lower cover square tools, depicting a horse-like dragon. Re-backed; traces of one pair of clasps.

This copy was one of three Caxton volumes bequeathed to the Bristol Baptist College with other early printed books by Andrew Gifford (1700–84), a numismatist, Baptist minister and assistant librarian at the British Museum. It was purchased by the Museum from the College in 1960. A fragment of printer's waste from Caxton's edition of the *Fifteen Oes* used as a paste-down is exhibited separately.

103 A binding by the 'Caxton binder', *c.*1490.
Dicts and sayings of the philosophers. Third edition.
Westminster: W. Caxton, [1489]. fol.
IB 55143.

Brown calf over wooden boards, tooled in blind to a panel design. The outer border contains carrot and nosegay tools and the panel is divided by fillets into lozenges containing nosegay tools, and half lozenges containing carrot tools. Re-backed; remnants of one pair of clasps.

104 A binding by the 'Caxton binder', *c.*1491.
J. Mirk: *Liber festivalis.* Second edition.
Westminster: W. Caxton, [1491]. fol.
IB 55146. (De Ricci 80:1)

Brown calf over wooden boards, tooled in blind to a panel design. The panel is divided by fillets into lozenges, containing large square griffin tools, and half lozenges containing carrot tools. Re-backed; remnants of one pair of clasps.

105 A binding by the 'Caxton binder', *c.*1493.
The Chastising of God's children.
Westminster: W. de Worde, [*c.*1492] and
Treatise of love.
Westminster: W. de Worde, [1493]. fol.
Lent by the Dean and Chapter of Lincoln Cathedral.

Brown leather over wooden boards, tooled in blind to a panel design. The panel is divided by fillets into lozenges containing lozenge-shaped nosegay tools, and half lozenges containing round fleur-de-lis tools. The outer border contains the same nosegay and fleur-de-lis tools. Re-backed; remnants of one pair of clasps.

106 A binding by the 'Caxton binder', *c.*1494.
Horae B.M.V. ad usum Sarum.
[Westminster:] W. de Worde, [*c.*1494]. 4°.
Lent by His Grace the Archbishop of Canterbury and the Trustees of Lambeth Palace Library.

Brown calf over wooden boards, tooled in blind with four identical panels, separated by a horizontal row of square floral tools. The panels depict birds and monkeys in foliage and are surrounded by the legend: 'sit nomen / domini benedictum / ex hoc nunc / et usque in seculum'. Re-backed; two pairs of clasps added later.

107 A binding by the 'Caxton binder', *c*.1485.

Bartholomaeus Platina: *Liber de vita Christi.*

Nuremberg: A. Koberger, 1481, and
W. Rolewinck: *Fasciculus temporum.* N.d. fol.

Lent by the Master and Fellows of Pembroke College, Cambridge.

Brown calf over wooden boards, tooled in blind to a panel design. The panel is divided by fillets into strips containing fleur-de-lis tools, and lozenges containing groups of four fleur-de-lis tools. Re-backed; traces of two pairs of clasps.

108 A binding by the 'Caxton binder', *c*.1504.

Joannes Balbus: *Catholicon.*

Lyons: N. Wolff, 1503. fol.

Lent by the President and Fellows of Corpus Christi College, Oxford.

Brown leather over wooden boards, tooled in blind to a panel design. The border of the panel is filled with triangular dragon tools and the panel is divided by fillets into lozenges, containing large square griffin tools and half lozenges, containing square floral tools. Spine: four double bands and five compartments; lettering piece added later; traces of three pairs of clasps.

109 A binding by the 'Caxton binder', *c*.1507.

Eusebius: *Historia ecclesiastica.*

Hagenau: H. Gran, 1506. fol.

British Library: Henry Davis Gift.

Brown leather over wooden board, tooled in blind to a panel design. The border of the panel is filled with interlaced crescent tools and the panel is divided by fillets into lozenges, containing square floral tools. Remnants of two pairs of clasps.

110 A binding by the 'Caxton binder', *c*.1507.

Horae B.M.V. ad usum Sarum.

Paris, for W. Bretton, 1506. 8°.

Lent by the Curators of the Bodleian Library.

Brown leather over wooden boards, tooled in blind with a border filled with interlaced crescent tools and two panels separated by a horizontal row of square floral tools. The panels depict birds and monkeys in foliage and are surrounded by the legend: 'sit nomen / domini benedictum / ex hoc nunc / et usque in seculum'. Re-backed; traces of three pairs of clasps.

[94]